Introduction to Our KS2 Ma~~ths~~ ~~Series~~

The central aim of Coordination Group Publications is to produce
top quality teaching and learning material which is carefully matched
to the National Curriculum, and then supply it as cheaply as possible.

These brilliant KS2 Maths Classbooks have *Three Top Features*:

Carefully Matched to the National Numeracy Strategy

*Underneath the humour and chatty style, we have written these books to
exactly match the National Numeracy Strategy Framework for each year.
The Classbooks follow the Recommended Yearly Teaching Programme,
and we've produced great Homework Books that run alongside them.*

Deliberate Use of Humour

*We like to include loads of funny bits and pictures instead of giving kids
boring lists of facts to learn. The jokes are there to keep kids reading and
to keep them alert for learning the important bits.*

They're Top Dollar Value

*These Classbooks have everything. They contain all the information
needed, they're printed in fabulous full colour, they've got loads of little
jolly bits in to tickle your humour buds — and they're a fabulous price.
That's top dollar value alright.*

Buy our books — they're ace

Where to Find What

These Classbooks have been carefully tailored to the Framework, so that they follow exactly the order of teaching for Year 4, as suggested in the Yearly Teaching Programme. Of course, this means that each topic is split into bite-size units. To make it easier to find what you want, we've grouped them together here under the five main strands.

SOLVING PROBLEMS

HANDLING DATA

MEASURES, SHAPE AND SPACE

Published by Coordination Group Publications

Co-edited by:
Glenn Rogers BSc (Hons)

Written and Illustrated by:
Paul Burton BSc (Hons)
Gemma Hallam BA (Hons)
Claire Thompson BSc
Andrew Wright BA (Hons)

Additional Illustrations:
James Paul Wallis BEng (Hons)
Lex Ward

Additional Writers:
Charley Darbishire BA (Hons)
Laura Schibrowski BSc (Hons)

With thanks to Claire Thompson for the Numeracy Strategy Research.

ISBN 1-84 146-053-2

Groovy website: www.cgpbooks.co.uk

Printed by Elanders Hindson Ltd., Newcastle upon Tyne.
Clipart sources: CorelDRAW and VECTOR.
0999

Large Numbers

4-digit numbers are pretty much like good old 3-digit numbers (they've got <u>hundreds</u>, <u>tens</u> and <u>units</u>) but now there's an extra column — the <u>thousands</u> column.

Numbers can be in Words or Figures

Write down 1256 in words.

1256 is written as one thousand, two hundred and fifty-six.

Write these numbers down in words:

1230 = ...

2435 = ...

4279 = ...

Simon has 1657 spots dotted about his body. How many is this in words?

....

....

Write these numbers down in figures:

One thousand, seven hundred and forty-three = ...

Six thousand, five hundred and ninety-eight = ...

Place Value for larger numbers

Learn the order the numbers go in: Thousands, hundreds, tens and units.

How much is the 3 worth in these numbers?
Is it three thousand, three hundred, thirty or just plain three?

1230	1350 ....
1563	3758 ....
4397	6736 ....

Ordering Large Numbers

Sort them by the <u>thousands</u> digit first, then the <u>hundreds</u>, then the <u>tens</u>, and then the <u>units</u>.

EXAMPLE: Order these numbers: 1474, 3478, 5486, 1456, 1234

(1) Look at the THOUSANDS digits first:

The green tick means you're sure about these.

? ? ?   ✓ ✓

<u>1</u>474, <u>1</u>456, <u>1</u>234, <u>3</u>478, <u>5</u>486.

Five thousand and something is bigger than three thousand and something.

You don't know yet which way round these three go.

(2) You need to look at the HUNDREDS digits to sort them out:

✓ ? ? ✓ ✓
1<u>2</u>34, 1<u>4</u>74, 1<u>4</u>56, 3478, 5486.

Four hundred and something is bigger than two hundred and something

(3) The TENS digits will sort the last two out:

✓ ✓ ✓ ✓ ✓
1234, 14<u>5</u>6, 14<u>7</u>4, 3478, 5486.

Seventy-something is bigger than fifty-something

Now have a go at ordering these sets of numbers:

2365, 4598, 3578, 1297, 5798   ....

2574, 2379, 1156, 3467, 3235   ....

5684, 5368, 865, 4768, 48   ....

3358, 253, 1589, 1526, 37   ....

Which of these numbers is biggest:

1245 or 1254? ....   3246 or 3462? ....

5689 or 5869? ....   7459 or 7954? ....

Willy has 3498 "Wacko" stickers and his mate Wayne has 3894 "Wildo" stickers. Who has the most stickers?

....

Halfway Points

If you need to work out the halfway point between
3400 and **3410**, you can do it in two ways:

1) Halfway points with a number line

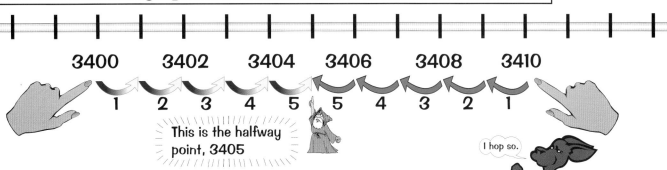

3400   **3402**   **3404**   **3406**   **3408**   **3410**

1   2   3   4   5   5   4   3   2   1

This is the halfway point, **3405**

I hop so.

① Start with <u>one finger</u> on <u>one</u> of the numbers, and a finger of your <u>other hand</u> on the <u>other number</u>.

② Take one finger-hop to the <u>right</u> from the <u>smallest</u> number, and at the same time take one hop to the <u>left</u> from the <u>largest</u> number.

Did somebody say hop?

③ <u>Keep hopping</u> like this until your fingers <u>meet</u>.

Use the number lines below to find the halfway points between these pairs of numbers:

2300 and 2400 ....

5600 and 5800 ....

2) Halfway points with Mental Calculations

The other way to find the halfway point between 2 numbers is to work out the <u>difference</u> between the numbers and add <u>half</u> the difference to the <u>smaller</u> number:

The difference between 3400 and 3410 is 10.
Half of 10 is 5.   And now 3400 + 5 = 3405.

Remember, finding the difference means doing a take-away sum.

Without using a number line, find the halfway points between these numbers:

4600 and 4700 ....

1500 and 1700 ....

2840 and 2940 ....

Measures, Shape and Space	# *Simple Number Lines*

Watch out! A mark on a scale isn't <u>always</u> one unit.
Some scales are marked in <u>twos</u>, <u>fives</u> or <u>tens</u>.

A Number Scale is Split into Steps

This number scale is marked in <u>twos</u>. Each mark on the number line is a step of 2:

0   20   40

What number is this arrow pointing to?

This arrow is pointing to a number <u>three steps</u> away from 20. Count down in <u>twos</u>. One step takes you to <u>18</u>, another step takes you to <u>16</u>, and a third step takes you to <u>14</u>. That's your answer.

First of all, work out the scale.
This one's marked in twos.
Next, count up or down in those steps.
For this question, you count up in twos.

Work out what numbers these arrows are pointing to:

30   50   70

....

Find the circled numbers on these number lines:

50   100   150

....

Now, this is a bit trickier.
These questions use <u>new</u> scales.
Here's how to work out how <u>big</u> the steps are on a scale.

Start with <u>two points</u> that have the numbers <u>already</u> written by them.
Find the <u>difference</u> between the two points (that means subtracting).
<u>Divide it</u> by the <u>number of marks</u> it takes to get from one point to the other.

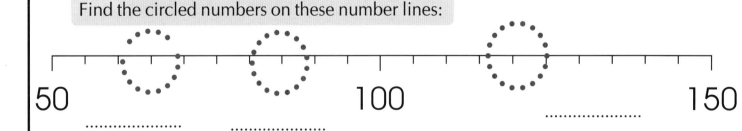

300   400   500

....

Reading Rulers

Rulers are just like Number Lines

You read <u>rulers</u> just like <u>number lines</u>. They've just got more marks on them.

EXAMPLE: What is the arrow pointing to on this ruler, to the nearest $\frac{1}{2}$ cm?

The arrow is between the marks for $3\frac{1}{2}$ and 4 cm. Decide which it's <u>closest to</u> and that's the <u>answer</u>. In this case it's closest to $3\frac{1}{2}$ cm.

Write down the points marked on this ruler:

One of the little marks is 1 mm, and the bigger marks are 0.5 cm.

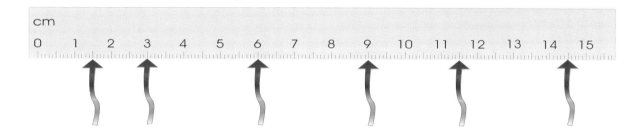

················ ················ ················ ················ ················ ················

Drawing Accurate Lines means reading a Ruler

If you want to draw a line of <u>exactly</u> $5\frac{1}{2}$ cm, you'll need to use a <u>ruler</u> and be able to read it properly. Here's how to do it.

(1) <u>Start</u> your line at the <u>0 cm mark</u>.

(2) Read carefully along to $5\frac{1}{2}$ cm (counting on <u>five</u> of the little <u>millimetre</u> marks).

(3) <u>Draw</u> your line from the 0 cm mark to the $5\frac{1}{2}$ cm point on the ruler.

<u>Don't</u> move the <u>ruler</u> when you're doing it, or it'll go completely <u>wrong</u>.

Draw and label a 5 mm, a 15 cm, a 7 cm and a 11 cm line in the space below:

Calculations	# Understanding +

You know how to <u>add</u> things up. Here are some <u>sums</u> to remind you.

35 + 74 = ...   91 + 16 = ...   54 + 45 = ...

Now have a look at these sums — they're the same numbers the <u>other way</u> round.

74 + 35 = ...   16 + 91 = ...   45 + 54 = ...

Remember — <u>addition</u> sums are the same either way round. **74 + 35** is the <u>same as</u> **35 + 74**.

Add 3 Numbers by Adding 2 Numbers Twice

EXAMPLE: What is 64 + 37 + 46?

Grrr... that looks pretty difficult to me.
But it's easier if you break it up into two little sums.

Look at it like this: (64 + 37) + **46**
First of all, add the first two numbers.

64 + 37 = 101

Now the sum is much easier.

101 + 46 = 147

It <u>doesn't matter</u> which <u>order</u> you put the sum in.

Check for yourself.

64 + (37 + 46) = 64 + ... = ...

Work out these sums by doing two little sums:

This time you decide which two numbers to add up first.

91 + 18 + 34 = ... + 34 = ...
                                   38 + 75 + 22 = ... + ... = ...

91 + 18 + 34 = 91 + ... = ...
                                     42 + 56 + 45 = ... + ... = ...

38 + 75 + 22 = 38 + ... = ...
                                     79 + 82 + 36 = ... + ... = ...

29 + 12 + 48 = 29 + ... = ...
                                     42 + 31 + 57 = ... + ... = ...

Understanding –

Subtraction means <u>taking away</u> one number from another. <u>Practise</u> with these.

$90 - 74 =$ ....

$54 - 32 =$ ....

$68 - 44 =$ ....

> You need to <u>remember</u> that subtraction is <u>not</u> like addition — the <u>order</u> does matter. **90 – 74** is <u>**NOT**</u> the same as **74 – 90**.

Take Away 2 Numbers One at a Time

Taking away <u>two numbers</u> looks horrible, but don't panic!
The big <u>mistake</u> is trying to do it <u>all</u> at once. <u>Break up</u> the sum and take away <u>one number</u> at a time. I've done the first one for you.

Not that kind of takeaway...

$89 - 24 - 31 = 89 - 24 - 31 =$ ....._65_.... $- 31 =$ ...._34_...

$136 - 34 - 62 = 136 - 34 - 62 =$ .... $- 62 =$ ....

$101 - 26 - 39 = 101 - 26 - 39 =$ .... $- 39 =$ ....

$98 - 56 - 17 = 98 - 56 - 17 =$ .... $- 39 =$ ....

But <u>watch out</u> — look <u>what happens</u> if you try to do it the <u>other way</u> round.

$120 - 35 - 23 = 120 - 35 - 23 = 120 - 12$..... **Oh, no it <u>doesn't</u>!**

You need to <u>add</u> the last two numbers, <u>not</u> take them away.

$120 - 35 - 23 = 120 - 35 + 23 = 120 -$ ...._58_.... $=$ ...._62_.... .

You're taking away <u>twice</u>, which means you're taking <u>more</u> away.
That's <u>why</u> you can <u>add</u> the last two numbers. You're taking a <u>bigger number</u> away.

Check for yourself — these pairs of sums have the same answer

$113 - 29 - 43 = 113 - 29 - 43 =$ .... $- 43 =$ ....

$113 - 29 - 43 = 113 - 29 + 43 = 113 -$ .... $=$ ....

Now try these:

$167 - 101 - 34 = 167 - 101 + 34 = 167 -$ .... $=$ ....

$91 - 23 - 41 = 91 - 23 + 41 = 91 -$ .... $=$ ....

Calculations

Mental Strategies

Split up Numbers into Tens and Units

Gerald is throwing a cocktail party and needs to work out <u>how many</u> olives he has. He has 37 olives in the <u>jar</u> and 52 in the <u>bowl</u>.

Here's a nice <u>easy</u> way to do the sum in your <u>head</u>.

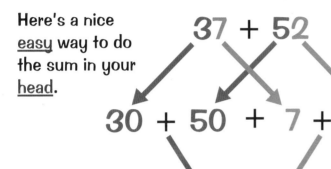

$$37 + 52$$

$$30 + 50 + 7 + 2$$

$$80 + 9 = 89$$

You can <u>subtract</u> this way, too. First take away the <u>tens</u>, then the <u>units</u>.
89 − 37 =
89 − 30 − 7 =
59 − 7 = 52.

Work out these sums by splitting into tens and units.

35 + 42 = <u>30 + 40</u> + <u>5 + 2</u> = <u>70</u> + <u>7</u> = <u>77</u>

66 + 83 = ... + ... = ... + ... = ...

59 + 33 = ... + ... = ... + ... = ...

29 + 76 = ... + ... = ... + ... = ...

74 + 61 = ... + ... = ... + ... = ...

Now try these subtractions — take away the tens first, then the units.

95 − 44 = 95 − <u>40</u> − <u>4</u> = <u>55</u> − <u>4</u> = <u>51</u>

78 − 35 = 78 − .... − .... = ... − .... = ...

56 − 22 = 56 − .... − .... = ... − .... = ...

64 − 51 = 64 − .... − .... = ... − .... = ...

88 − 32 = 88 − .... − .... = ... − .... = ...

Taking away the tens first and then the units makes it so much easier.

Mental Strategies

Add up Numbers that are Close Together

Here's an <u>easy</u> way to do hard-looking sums with <u>big</u> numbers.

305 + 297

Hmm. Something looks <u>interesting</u> — they're both very close to <u>300</u>.

300 + 5   300 – 3

Now we can <u>split</u> it up into sums that are much more <u>simple</u>.

300 + 300 + 5 – 3 = 600 + 5 – 3 = **602**

Split these numbers up to make the sums easier:

599 + 603 = *600 – 1+ 600 + 3* = *1200 – 1 + 3* = *1202*

406 + 397 = ... + ... = ... = ...

998 + 1004 = ... + ... = ... = ...

1995 + 2004 = ... + ... = ... = ...

501 + 495 = ... + ... = ... = ...

<u>Careful</u> with the last two — you need to <u>take away</u> more than you <u>add</u>.

Take away Numbers that are Close Together

When you have to <u>subtract</u> big numbers, the <u>best</u> way is simply to <u>count up</u> from the smaller one. If there's a hundred or a thousand in the middle, it's a useful rest stop.

EXAMPLE: 1005 – 997.

① You know that it's 3 from 997 to 1000.

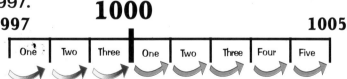
997 **1000** **1005**
One | Two | Three | One | Two | Three | Four | Five

② You know that it's 5 from 1000 to 1005.

③ Add them together to get 8.

1005 – 997 = 8.

Count up from the smaller number to get the answer to these sums:

403 – 399 = ...   710 – 698 = ...

1006 – 994 = ...   6001 – 5993 = ...

4001 – 3996 = ...   909 – 898 = ...

Calculations

Pencil and Paper Procedures

Add to Numbers with Three Digits

Alf and his mum have been picking <u>strawberries</u>.
His mum only picked <u>86</u>, but Alf picked <u>348</u>.
How <u>many</u> did they pick in total?

The <u>easy</u> way to do it is
<u>one step</u> at a time.

$$348$$
$$+ \ 86$$

First the <u>hundreds</u> ⟶ 300

Now the <u>tens</u> 40 + 80 ⟶ +120

Finally the <u>units</u> 8 + 6 ⟶ + 14

These are <u>much easier</u> numbers to add up. **434**

Add the hundreds, tens then units to make these sums easier.

485	724	379	164
+ 77	+ 46	+ 39	+ 83

400
+ 150
+ 12
562

756	877	336	606
+ 49	+ 66	+ 73	+ 58

You don't <u>have</u> to use different <u>colours</u> for the hundreds, tens and units — I've only done it to help you remember <u>which is which</u>.

Pencil and Paper Procedures

Take Away from a Three-Digit Number

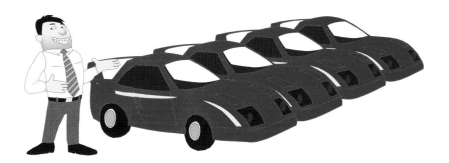

This is <u>Honest Jim</u>. At the start of the month he had 624 <u>cars</u> in his <u>used car lot</u>. Since then he's <u>sold</u> 57 of them. How <u>many</u> does he have <u>left</u>?

Looks pretty <u>tricky</u> to me — but I'll show you an <u>easy</u> way. <u>Count up</u> from the <u>lower</u> number to the <u>bigger</u> one in stages. You're trying to get to a nice plain round number each time.

624

− 57

This is the sum you have to do.

First of all, add <u>3</u> to 57 to get <u>60</u>   ➤   **3**   gets you to 60

Now, to get to <u>100</u> from 60 add <u>40</u>   ➤   **40**   gets you to 100

To get from 100 to <u>600</u> add <u>500</u>   ➤   **500**   gets you to 600

Nearly there. Adding <u>20</u> takes you to <u>620</u>   ➤   **20**   gets you to 620

Hurrah. Adding another <u>4</u> gets you to <u>624</u>   ➤   **4**   gets you to 624

<u>Add up</u> the numbers that took us from <u>57</u> to <u>624</u> and we get   **567**

And that's the <u>answer!</u>

Try these subtraction sums by counting up from the smaller number to the big one.

486	514	761	934	252
− 69	− 55	− 81	− 62	− 78

Happy, Grumpy, Sleepy — they're 3-MIDGETS...

Remember — when you've got to <u>add</u> or <u>subtract</u> with three-digit numbers, it's much easier if you <u>break</u> the numbers up into <u>hundreds</u>, <u>tens</u> and <u>units</u>.

Solving Problems

Real Life

Sometimes you won't just be <u>told</u> to do a sum.
You'll be given a question and <u>you'll</u> have to notice that you need to do a sum — and you'll have to work out <u>what</u> it is.

Solve Problems about Numbers in Real Life

EXAMPLE: Lucy guzzles 46 chocolate doughnuts for <u>breakfast</u>, 93 for <u>lunch</u> and 137 for <u>dinner</u>. How many chocolate doughnuts does Lucy eat during the <u>whole day</u>?

<u>ANSWER</u>: looks like an <u>addition</u> problem to me. We need to <u>add up</u> 46, 93 and 137.

$$46 + 93 + 137 = 276$$

EXAMPLE: Johnboy has to <u>shovel</u> 234 haystacks to earn his pocket money. He's <u>already</u> shovelled 62 of them. How many <u>more</u> haystacks does he have to shovel?

<u>ANSWER</u>: Hmm. Looks like a <u>subtraction</u> problem. We need to <u>take away</u> 62 from 234.

$$234 - 62 = 172$$

Decide whether you need to add up or take away and do the sum.

Mohammed thinks of a number, then subtracts 25. He's left with 42. What is the number that Mohammed thought of?

The sum you need to do is .... and the answer is ....

Jane has 38 fewer toy cars than Alex. If Alex has 104 toy cars, how many does Jane have?

The sum you need to do is .... and the answer is ....

Real Life

Time to Practise those Real Life Problems

Helen sets off to drive 212 miles to visit her friend Ian. After 83 miles she stops for a cup of coffee. How many more miles does she have to drive?

Write the sum and the answer here ....

Billy weighed 70 kg before he took part in the World Cake-Eating Championships. He weighs 107 kg afterwards. How many kg of weight has Billy gained?

....

Postman Pete delivered 312 letters on his first round and 89 on his second round. How many letters has he delivered in all this morning?

....

Terry the Toucan likes his tea. He got 250 tea bags at the weekend and now he only has 72 left. How many teabags has he used?

....

Jasmine has 159 books on her bookshelves and 42 books on her table. She lends 19 books to her friend Sarah. How many books does she have now?

HINT: you need to add and subtract things here.

....

Natalie is training for a marshmallow marathon. She has run 140 miles this month, she ran 97 miles last month and 76 miles the month before that. How many miles has she run in total in the last three months?

....

Solving Problems

Checking Results

Check by Adding in a Different Order

It doesn't matter what <u>order</u> you add numbers in. So you can <u>check</u> <u>your answer</u> by adding the same numbers in a <u>different</u> order.

$9 + 7 + 4 = 20$

<u>Check</u> the answer by doing <u>one of</u> these sums.

$4 + 7 + 9 =$ ......

$7 + 4 + 9 =$ ......

$4 + 9 + 7 =$ ......

$7 + 9 + 4 =$ ......

$9 + 4 + 7 =$ ......

This is a <u>useful trick</u>. If you get a <u>different</u> answer the second time round, you know you've done one of them <u>wrong</u>.

Check these sums by adding the numbers in a different order.

$25 + 48 + 187 = 25 +$ .....*235*..... $=$ .....*260*.....

$187 + 48 + 25 = 187 +$ .... $=$ ....

$82 + 291 + 43 = 82 +$ .... $=$ ....

$43 + 291 + 82 = 43 +$ .... $=$ ....

$5 + 7 + 9 + 1 =$ .... $1 + 9 + 7 + 5 =$ ....

$12 + 5 + 7 + 3 =$ .... $3 + 7 + 5 + 12 =$ ....

Jim has baked a batch of 24 ham and sprout buns. He has another 32 in the oven, and 46 waiting to go in. How many buns will he end up with?

Write out the sum and add it up.   .... $+$ .... $+$ .... $=$ ....

Now check your answer by adding the numbers in a different order.   .... $+$ .... $+$ .... $=$ ....

Checking Results

Check by doing an Equivalent Calculation

You can often do the <u>same sum</u> in lots of ways.

Try these <u>three</u> different ways of doing this <u>one</u> sum.

140 + 136

Because I'm nice, I've done the first one for you. There's no need to thank me...

$140 + 140 - 4 = \underset{\dots\dots}{280} - 4 = \underset{\dots\dots}{276}$

$140 + 130 + 6 = \dots\dots + 6 = \dots\dots$

$100 + 100 + 40 + 36 = 200 + \dots\dots = \dots\dots$

Check your answers to these sums by doing them in more than one way.

$245 + 251 = 250 + 250 - 5 + 1 = \dots\dots - 5 + 1 = \dots\dots$

$245 + 251 = 240 + 250 + 5 + 1 = \dots\dots + 5 + 1 = \dots\dots$

$245 + 251 = 200 + 200 + 45 + 51 = 400 + \dots\dots = \dots\dots$

$89 + 92 = 90 + 90 - 1 + 2 = \dots\dots - 1 + 2 = \dots\dots$

$89 + 92 = 80 + 90 + 9 + 2 = \dots\dots + 9 + 2 = \dots\dots$

Don't panic! If you've done everything on these two pages, you'll be able to do this.

Find three different ways of doing this sum

$118 + 126 = \dots\dots\dots\dots\dots\dots\dots = \dots\dots$

or $\dots\dots\dots\dots\dots\dots\dots = \dots\dots$

or $\dots\dots\dots\dots\dots\dots\dots = \dots\dots$

Check your Answers — Spotty Ones look awful...

It's easy to make a <u>mistake</u> — so it's always a good idea to check you've done a sum <u>correctly</u> by doing it in a different way. If you get the same answer, it's probably <u>right</u>.

Units

Units of Weight are g and kg

If you want to find the weight of an object you could use a set of <u>weighing scales</u>.

A heavy object is weighed in kilograms, and a light one in grams.

Which of these units is a unit of weight: ml, g, m, cm, pint, kilometre, kg?

....

Units of Length are mm, cm, m, km and miles

If you want to find the <u>length</u> of an object you could use a ruler.

(If the object was a mile long, it would have to be a big ruler!)
You also use these units to say how <u>far away</u> something is.

A <u>small</u> object is measured in <u>mm</u> or <u>cm</u>.
A person's height is measured in <u>cm</u> or <u>m</u>, and a very <u>long</u> distance is measured in <u>km</u> or <u>miles</u>.

Which of these units is a unit of length: mm, g, m, cm, l, gram, ml, km?

....

Units of Capacity are ml, l and pints

Capacity is the <u>amount</u> of <u>stuff</u> things like bottles or buckets can <u>hold</u>.

The units for capacity are <u>millilitres</u> (ml), <u>litres</u> (l) and <u>pints</u>.

The capacity of a small bottle is measured in <u>ml</u>. A large bucket is measured in <u>litres</u>.
<u>Pints</u> are an <u>old</u> unit and are used to measure the capacity of bottles of <u>milk</u>.

Which of these units is a unit of capacity: cm, pint, kg, ml, l, g, m, mile?

....

Mark wants to measure the length of his cricket bat. Which of these units should he use: ml, pints, miles, cm, kg, grams?

....

If he wants to weigh his bat, which of the units should he use?

....

Measuring Things

Decide which Units to use

What units would you use to measure the length of a fly?

Is a fly small, big or in the middle?
It's <u>small</u>, so we would measure the length of it in <u>mm</u>.

What units would you measure the length of a car in? ....

What units would you measure the distance from Cardiff to London in? ....

What units could you measure the capacity of a mug in? ....

What units would you use for these:

the length of a spider? ....   the capacity of a teaspoon? ....

the weight of a chocolate bar? ....

the weight of a man? ....   the capacity of a bucket? ....

Decide what to measure with

EXAMPLE: What would you measure the weight of a cup cake with?

A cup cake is fairly light, so you would probably use some <u>kitchen scales</u>.
If you were weighing something heavier then you would use a set of
<u>bathroom scales</u>.

What would you use to measure the weight of a chair? ....

What would you use to measure the length of an ant? ....

What would you use to measure the length of a table? ....

What would you use to measure the length of a house? ....

If you're measuring the <u>capacity</u> of something, use a measuring jug or cylinder.

If you're measuring the length of something small, use a ruler. If it's something large use a tape measure. If it's somewhere in the middle use a metre rule.

What would you use to measure the capacity of a bucket? ....

What would you use to measure the capacity of a cola bottle? ....

Shapes

Two-Dimensional Shapes are Flat

Here are some shapes and their names.
Write the correct name next to each shape.

Isosceles Triangle

Heptagon   Pentagon

Square
                                    Oblong
Hexagon   Circle

                        Octagon
          Semicircle

Equilateral Triangle

These are funny looking words, but you need to <u>know</u> them.

....

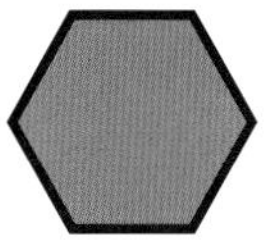

....

....

....

....

....

....

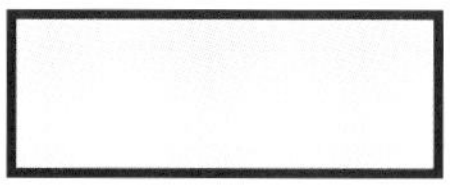

....

....

....

Now say what kind of shapes these groups are.

Fill in the gaps with one of these words: _triangles_   _polygons_   _rectangles_

Because they have

three sides, these

shapes are both ....

An oblong and

a square are

both ....

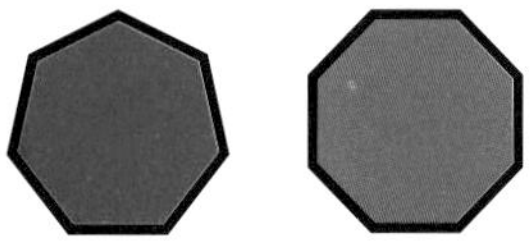

Triangles and shapes with more than

three sides are all ....

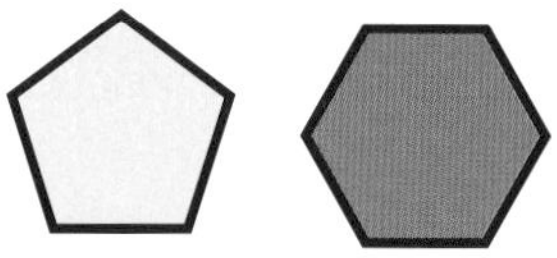

3D Shapes

Three-Dimensional Shapes are Solid

Here are some three-dimensional shapes and their names. Write the correct name next to each shape.

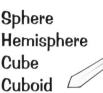

Sphere
Hemisphere
Cube
Cuboid
Triangular Prism
Cylinder

....

....

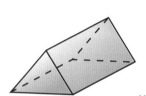

....

....

....

....

Which shapes fit into which group?

Use these facts to help you.

A 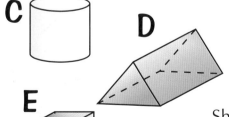 **B**

A <u>Pyramid</u> has triangular faces that come up from its base and meet in a <u>point</u> at the top.

A <u>Polyhedron</u> has sides which are all flat and all <u>polygons</u>.

A <u>Tetrahedron</u> has four faces.

C

D

Ouch, more long words... Learn them, then they won't seem as bad.

A <u>Prism</u> has the same flat shape running all the way through it.

E

Shapes ...*A*... and ...*B*... are both pyramids.

Only shape .... is a tetrahedron.

Shapes ...., ... and .... are all prisms.

Shapes ...., ..., ... and .... are polyhedrons.

Polygons

A Polygon is a Flat Shape with 3 or more Sides

A Polygon is a closed shape — the lines join up.
It's a flat shape.
It's got three or more sides.
All the sides are straight. Whew — got that?

Are these shapes polygons?

All those things have got to be true for the shape to be a polygon.

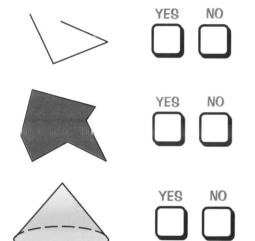

YES   NO

YES   NO

YES   NO

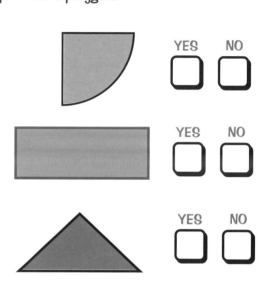

YES   NO

YES   NO

YES   NO

Regular Polygons have Equal Sides and Angles

As if you didn't have enough funny words to remember, here's another one — regular polygon. That's a polygon with sides all the same length, and angles which are all the same too.

Both those things have got to be true for the shape to be a regular polygon.

Put a tick under the regular polygons.

....

You should recognise these two shapes — a square and an equilateral triangle. They're both regular polygons.

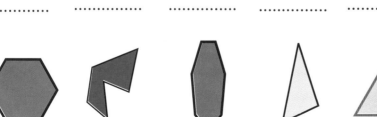

....

Polyhedrons

A Polyhedron is made up of Polygons

A Polyhedron is made up of polygons.

Each of the four faces of this polyhedron is flat, and a polygon.

Pretty Polyhedron

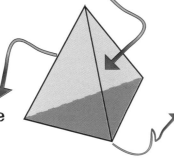

Each edge is a straight line where two faces meet.

And here's another silly word — vertex. Where three or more edges meet, you get a vertex.

Don't worry — vertex is just the maths word for corner.

A regular polyhedron has regular polygons for sides. Makes sense, really...

This is NOT a polyhedron. You can tell because the base is not a polygon — it's a circle. The sides are curvy, not flat.

Are these shapes polyhedrons or not?

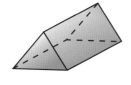   YES ☐ NO ☐

   YES ☐ NO ☐

   YES ☐ NO ☐

   YES ☐ NO ☐

Remember, a shape isn't a polyhedron just because it's solid. Check the facts at the top of the page.

   YES ☐ NO ☐

   YES ☐ NO ☐

Who's in good shape? — Paul, he'd run...

Polygons and polyhedrons — it could get a bit confusing if you're not careful, so get it sorted. Polygons are the flat shapes and polyhedrons are the big chunky solid shapes. Remember — two-dimensional means flat and three-dimensional means solid.

Solving Problems	# 3D Shape Problems

How many Cubes are in these Shapes?

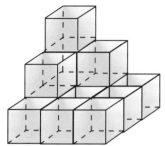

Here's an exciting <u>3-D shape</u>. How many of these <u>cubes</u> would you need to make it?

Imagine <u>building</u> this shape from cubes and you can come up with the <u>answer</u>.

<u>One</u> on the top

<u>Three</u> here

And <u>nine</u> on the bottom layer

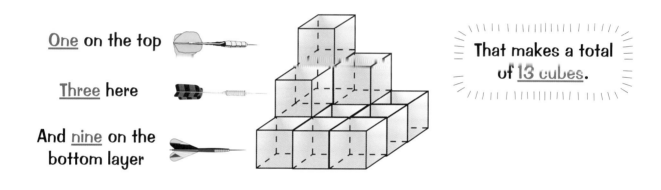

That makes a total of 13 cubes.

Try these: How many cubes would you need to build these shapes?

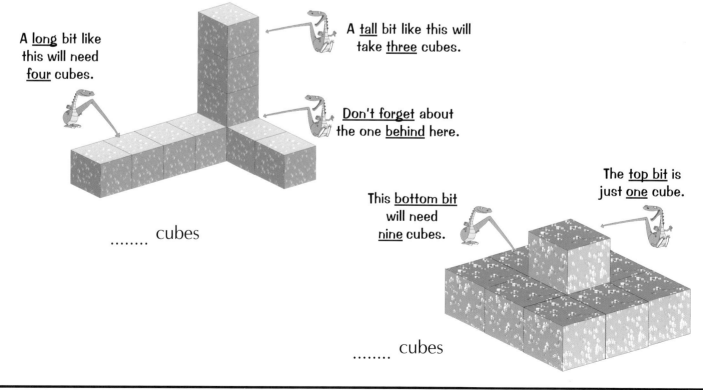

A <u>long</u> bit like this will need <u>four</u> cubes.

A <u>tall</u> bit like this will take <u>three</u> cubes.

<u>Don't forget</u> about the one <u>behind</u> here.

.... cubes

This <u>bottom bit</u> will need <u>nine</u> cubes.

The <u>top bit</u> is just <u>one</u> cube.

.... cubes

3D Shape Problems

.... cubes

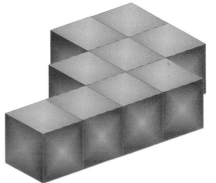

.... cubes

.... cubes

Watch out! There are some cubes that you can't see.

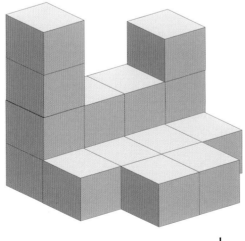

.... cubes

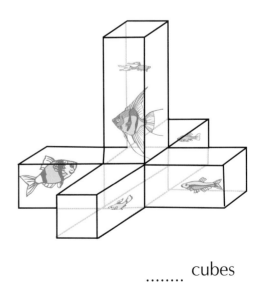

.... cubes

Numbers and the Number System

Simple Addition Patterns

Add the Same Number each time

EXAMPLE: What are the next four numbers in this sequence:

15,   18,   21,   24,   27,   *30*,   *33*, ..., ...,

+3   +3   +3   +3   +3

First, find the number that's being added each time to make the sequence.

Then add this number every time you want the next number in the sequence.

Fill in the last two numbers yourself.

Fill in the missing numbers in these sequences:

22,   25,   28,   31,   34, ..., ..., ..., ...

14,   18,   22,   26,   30, ..., ..., ..., ...

17,   22,   27,   32,   37, ..., ..., ..., ...

23, ...,   37,   44, +7 = *51*,   58,   65, ..., ...

+7   +7   +7

When you get one like this, find all the differences you can:

Then add the difference to a number you know to find one of the missing numbers:

To check it's right, all these differences should be the same.

Now fill in the missing numbers in these sequences:

12,   18, ...,   30, ...,   42,   48, ..., ...

45, ...,   59,   66, ...,   80,   87,   94, ...

17, ..., ...,   32,   37, ...,   47, ..., ...

.....,   28, ...,   46,   55, ...,   73,   82,   91

Quincy has a big mole problem. On Monday there were 12 moles in his garden, then there were more, and more...

Fill in the number of moles for the next 3 days.

Day	Mon	Tues	Wed	Thurs	Fri	Sat	Sun	Mon	Tues
Number of moles	12	21	30	39	48	57			

Simple Subtraction Patterns

Subtract the _Same Number_ each time

Fill in the next 4 numbers in this sequence:

Fill in the last 3 yourself.

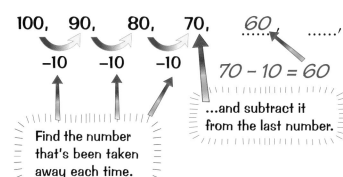

100,   90,   80,   70,   *60*, ..., ..., ...

−10   −10   −10

70 − 10 = 60

...and subtract it from the last number.

Find the number that's been taken away each time.

No, it said <u>subtract</u>, not <u>submarine</u>...

Add the next four terms to these sequences.

130,   121,   112,   103,   94, ..., ..., ..., ...

165,   162,   159,   156,   153, ..., ..., ..., ...

96,   89,   82,   74,   67, ..., ..., ..., ...

76,   71,   66,   61,   56, ..., ..., ..., ...

Now fill in the missing numbers in these sequences:

180,   173, ...,   159, ...,   145,   138, ..., ...

160,   157, ...,   151,   148, ...,   142, ...,   136

.......,   134, ...,   122,   116,   110, ..., ...,   92

65, ..., ...,   53,   49, ...,   41, ..., ...

Follow the steps on the previous page for these questions.

David has trouble with ants. He has 145 in his house.

When he uses Ace Ant Spray, the number of ants in his house goes down.

Fill in the table for the next 4 days of using the spray.

Day	Sat	Sun	Mon	Tues	Wed	Thurs	Fri	Sat	Sun
Number of ants	145	139	133	127	121				

Addition & Subtraction Patterns

Number patterns can help with sums

Look at the number patterns and then use them to answer these questions:

$5 + 12 = 17$

$15 + 12 = 27$

$25 + 12 = 37$

$35 + 12 = \text{....}$

$8 + 15 = 23$

$18 + 15 = 33$

$28 + 15 = 43$

$38 + 15 = \text{....}$

1) What is $68 + 15$?
2) What is $85 + 12$?

Both the questions fit into one of these <u>number patterns</u>.

$68 + 15$ fits in with this pattern. The <u>answer</u> must end in <u>3</u> like all the <u>others</u>.

If you follow the number pattern to $68 + 15$ you'll get an answer of 83.

Complete the two number patterns above.

Work out the answer to $85 + 12$, and write it here: ....

Answer these questions using the number patterns for help:

$55 + 12 =$ ....

$65 + 12 =$ ....

$78 + 15 =$ ....

$48 + 15 =$ ....

Use this number pattern to work out $48 - 11$.

$48 - 11$ fits into this number pattern. The <u>next sum</u> in the pattern is $58 - 11 = 47$, and the one <u>after</u> that is $48 - 11 = 37$. So, the answer is 37. Not so hard, really.

Write down the next 4 sums in the pattern:

....

....

$98 - 11 = 87$

$88 - 11 = 77$

$78 - 11 = 67$

$68 - 11 = 57$

Work out these sums:

$138 - 11 =$ ....

$18 - 11 =$ ....

$158 - 11 =$ ....

$118 - 11 =$ ....

$108 - 11 =$ ....

$128 - 11 =$ ....

There's <u>nothing</u> of any use over there.

Multiply and Divide with 0 and 1   Calculations

If you × or ÷ by 1, you get The Same Number

If you <u>multiply</u> or <u>divide</u> by 1 then you get the same number you started with.

EXAMPLE: What is 34×1?   **Answer: 34.**   It's as simple as that.

Answer these questions:

$38 \times 1 =$ .... $\qquad$ $43 \times 1 =$ .... $\qquad$ $64 \times 1 =$ ....

$124 \times 1 =$ .... $\qquad$ $58 \times 1 =$ .... $\qquad$ $1 \times 1 =$ ....

$589 \times 1 =$ .... $\qquad$ $99 \times 1 =$ .... $\qquad$ $5436 \times 1 =$ ....

$978 \times 1 =$ .... $\qquad$ $23 \times 1 =$ .... $\qquad$ $45 \times 1 =$ ....

$23 \div 1 =$ _23_ $\qquad$ $78 \div 1 =$ .... $\qquad$ $90 \div 1 =$ ....

Dividing by 1 gives the same result.
So even $3\ 756\ 683 \div 1$ is a dead easy sum.

Yup, this is boring...

If you Multiply by 0 you get Zero

Nope, nothing here worth looking at, nothing at all...

This is pretty <u>obvious</u> if you think about it.
If you multiply a number by <u>nothing</u>, then
what are you likely to get? — <u>nothing</u>.

Answer these questions:

$44 \times 0 =$ .... $\qquad$ $56 \times 0 =$ .... $\qquad$ $74 \times 0 =$ ....

$967 \times 0 =$ .... $\qquad$ $23 \times 0 =$ .... $\qquad$ $1 \times 0 =$ ....

$254 \times 0 =$ .... $\qquad$ $98 \times 0 =$ .... $\qquad$ $9067 \times 0 =$ ....

$175 \times 0 =$ .... $\qquad$ $11 \times 0 =$ .... $\qquad$ $36 \times 0 =$ ....

$111 \times 0 =$ .... $\qquad$ $23 \times 0 =$ .... $\qquad$ $5 \times 0.0 =$ ....

What's after the Nineties — the Nought-ies?...

This doesn't seem like anything terribly exciting, I admit. Remember that 5 x 1 means
<u>one</u> lot of five. 5 x 0 means <u>no</u> lots of five. Learn that, and you won't ever get caught out.

Calculations

The Order of × Doesn't Matter

Multiplication is the Same in Any Order

When you <u>times</u> numbers together, it <u>doesn't matter</u> what order you do them in.

<u>Three</u> lots of <u>four</u> beans is the same as four lots of three beans.
You've got <u>twelve</u> beans whichever way you look at it.

I'm full of beans

In numbers, $\underline{3 \times 4 = 4 \times 3 = 12}$.

Work out these sums. When the numbers are the same, the answers should be the same as well.

13 x 5 = ...   27 x 4 = ...   19 x 7 = ...

5 x 13 = ...   4 x 27 = ...   7 x 19 = ...

Work out the bit in purple first.

16 x 2 x 6 = 16 x 2 x 6 = ... x 6 = ...

16 x 2 x 6 = 16 x 2 x 6 = 16 x .... = ...

2 x 16 x 6 = 2 x 16 x 6 = 2 x .... = ...

6 x 16 x 2 = 6 x 16 x 2 = ... x 2 = ...

Once you've done this little lot, you'll see that it doesn't matter what order the numbers are in.

Gerald is trying to decide whether to buy 12 boxes of 24 chocolates or 24 boxes of 12 chocolates.

12 x 24 = ... and 24 x 12 = ...

So whichever he decides to buy, Gerald will get

.... chocolates.

The Order of ÷ Does Matter

Calculations

Number Order matters in Division

If you change the order of the numbers in a division sum, you'll get a <u>different answer</u>.

I've got a share of a million pounds divided between five people!

I've got a share of five pounds divided between a million people.

Division is <u>not</u> the same as multiplication. It matters <u>an awful lot</u> which way round the numbers go.

Five divided by a million... It's not the same as a million divided by five.

See for yourself by doing these sums.

5 ÷ 10 = ...   6 ÷ 60 = ...   2 ÷ 8 = ...

10 ÷ 5 = ...   60 ÷ 6 = ...   8 ÷ 2 = ...

It's the <u>same</u> with two-step division sums. The order you do them in really <u>matters</u>.

40 ÷ 8 ÷ 2 = ... *5* ..... ÷ 2 = ... *25* .....

40 ÷ 8 ÷ 2 = 40 ÷ ..... *4* ..... = ... *10* .....

50 ÷ 10 ÷ 2 = ... ÷ 2 = ...

50 ÷ 10 ÷ 2 = 50 ÷ .... = ...

80 ÷ 8 ÷ 4 = ... ÷ 4 = ...

80 ÷ 8 ÷ 4 = 80 ÷ .... = ...

Get your Orders in Order...

The order of numbers <u>doesn't</u> matter in <u>multiplication</u> — but it <u>does</u> matter in <u>division</u>. It's mega important you <u>remember</u> that and don't get the two <u>confused</u>.

Calculations	*Times Tables*

Know your 2, 3, 4, 5 and 10 Times Tables

You should already <u>know</u> what these are —
times tables are a <u>quick</u> way of learning how
to do multiplication sums.

My friend here thinks he's a genius.

I know the 1 times table all the way up to 5.

I know they're <u>boring</u> — but it's
definitely <u>worth</u> the effort.
When you <u>know</u> your times tables
you can do multiplication sums
quickly in your <u>head</u> — and people
will think you're dead <u>clever</u>.

	1	2	3	4	5	6	7	8	9	10
2 times table →	2	4	6	8	10	12	14	16	18	20
3 times table →	3	6	9	12	15	18	21	24	27	30
4 times table →	4	8	12	16	20	24	28	32	36	40
5 times table →	5	10	15	20	25	30	35	40	45	50
10 times table →	10	20	30	40	50	60	70	80	90	100

Do these as quickly as you can — you shouldn't really need to think about them.

5 x 5 = ...

4 x 7 = ...

3 x 4 = ...

2 x 9 = ...

10 x 10 = ...

5 x 2 = ...

10 x 8 = ...

4 x 6 = ...

2 x 4 = ...

3 x 8 = ...

2 x 3 = ...

3 x 7 = ...

10 x 4 = ...

5 x 6 = ...

4 x 10 = ...

9 x 3 = ...

7 x 5 = ...

8 x 2 = ...

6 x 10 = ...

7 x 4 = ...

Remember — <u>multiplication</u>
sums are the same in <u>any order</u>.
9 x 3 might look like the
<u>9 times</u> table — but switch the
numbers round and it's <u>3 x 9</u>,
in the <u>3 times table</u>.

Times Tables

Learn the 6, 7, 8 and 9 Times Tables

These are a bit more <u>difficult</u> to remember because they have <u>bigger</u> numbers.
But give it a go — you should be <u>quite quick</u> at answering these questions.
It's okay if you have to <u>think</u> for a bit <u>longer</u> than you do with smaller numbers.

That's not what I meant by six times table.

	1	2	3	4	5	6	7	8	9	10
6 times table ➡	6	12	18	24	30	36	42	48	54	60
7 times table ➡	7	14	21	28	35	42	49	56	63	70
8 times table ➡	8	16	24	32	40	48	56	64	72	80
9 times table ➡	9	18	27	36	45	54	63	72	81	90

Answer these sums as quickly as you can.

8 x 7 = ...

7 x 6 = ...

9 x 10 = ...

7 x 7 = ...

6 x 5 = ...

9 x 8 = ...

7 x 9 = ...

6 x 6 = ...

7 x 10 = ...

8 x 5 = ...

8 x 8 = ...

6 x 8 = ...

9 x 9 = ...

7 x 4 = ...

8 x 3 = ...

Calculations	**Multiplication by 4 and 8**

Use Doubling to Multiply by 4 and 8

Doubling and multiplying by four and eight go together like bananas and custard.

Double once → Double twice → Double again

Times by two   Times by four   Times by eight

Doubling something twice is an easy way of multiplying by four.
Multiplying by four then doubling is an easy way of multiplying by eight.

Use doubling to work out these sums.

Double 19 is *38* and double *38* is *76* , so 4 x 19 = *76*

Double 15 is .... and double .... is ...., so 4 x 15 = ...

Double 26 is .... and double .... is ...., so 4 x 26 = ...

Four times 12 is *48* and double *48* is *96* , so 8 x 12 = *96*

Four times 15 is .... and double .... is ...., so 8 x 15 = ...

Four times 21 is .... and double .... is ...., so 8 x 21 = ...

Finish off these sums to show what happens when you multiply by 4 then double.

4 x 1 = *4*	8 x 1 = *2 x 4* = *8*		4 x 6 = ...	8 x 6 = ...	= ....
4 x 2 = *8*	8 x 2 = *2 x 8* = *16*		4 x 7 = ...	8 x 7 = ...	= ....
4 x 3 = *12*	8 x 3 = *2 x 12* = *24*		4 x 8 = ...	8 x 8 = ...	= ....
4 x 4 = ...	8 x 4 = *2 x* = ...		4 x 9 = ...	8 x 9 = ...	= ....
4 x 5 = ...	8 x 5 = ... = ...		4 x 10 = ...	8 x 10 = ...	= ....

Multiplication by 5 and 20

Work Out × 5 and × 20 from × 10

You know it's <u>really easy</u> to multiply something by <u>10</u> — all you do is put a <u>nought</u> on the end. You can <u>use</u> that as the start of an easy way to do <u>x 5</u> or <u>x 20</u>.

To <u>multiply by 5</u>   First of all multiply by <u>10</u>   Then <u>divide by 2</u>

35 x 5 ➝ **35 x 10 = 350** ➝ **350 ÷ 2 = 175**

To <u>multiply by 20</u>   First of all multiply by <u>10</u>   Then <u>multiply by 2</u>

13 x 20 ══ **13 x 10 = 130** ══ **130 x 2 = 260**

It <u>makes sense</u> when you think about it. 5 is <u>10 ÷ 2</u> and 20 is <u>10 x 2</u>. That's a <u>good way</u> to remember it.

Do these sums by multiplying by ten then halving or doubling.

43 x 5 ➡ 43 x 10 = *430* and *430 ÷ 2* = *215*

22 x 20 ➡ 22 x 10 = *220* and *220 x 2* = *440*

36 x 5 ➡ 36 x 10 = ... and .... = ...

17 x 20 ➡ 17 x 10 = ... and .... = ...

29 x 20 ➡ 29 x 10 = ... and .... = ...

52 x 5 ➡ 52 x 10 = ... and .... = ...

60 x 5 ➡ 60 x 10 = ... and .... = ...

31 x 20 ➡ 31 x 10 = ... and .... = ...

25 x 5 ➡ 25 x 10 = ... and .... = ...

Hard Sums? — I prefer soft centred ones...

Multiplications that look <u>big</u> and <u>difficult</u> are easier if you do them in <u>two easy little bits</u>. Remember those tricks and you'll be able to multiply by 4, 5, 8 or 20 with no worries.

| Calculations | # Approximating Multiplication |

Do an Approximation for Difficult Sums

Before you do a big and scary sum, it's sometimes useful to do an approximation. This means you do a sum that's similar but easier.

23 x 8 ⟶ approximately 20 x 10 = 200

23 x 8 is a difficult sum. But 23 is near 20 and 8 is near 10, and 20 x 10 is easy. Working out that 20 x 10 = 200 gives us an approximation of the answer to 23 x 8.

We know that it's going to be somewhere near 200. That's useful because if we get an answer a long way away from 200, we'll know we've done the sum wrong.

Use the Grid Method to make a Sum Simpler

23 x 8 looks hard, but you can make it nice and easy. Split the 23 into 20 and 3, multiply the 20 and the 3 by 8 separately and then add up the results.

23 x 8 ⟶

x	20	3	
8	160	24	= 184

The answer is 184. And sure enough, that's quite close to our approximation of 200.

> Make an approximation then use the grid method to do these sums.

29 x 9 is approximately *30 x 10* which is *300* .

x	20	9	
9	180	81	= 261

47 x 6 is approximately .... which is ....

x	40	7	
6			= ....

33 x 8 is approximately .... which is ....

x	....	......	
....			= ....

62 x 4 is approximately .... which is ....

x	....	......	
....			= ....

...nating Division

Yo ...pprc ...tion for Division sums

It's also <u>useful</u> sometimes to d ... e difficult <u>division</u> sums,
to check your answer is in th... ... ...it <u>different</u>.

$$72 \div 5$$

$$50 \div 5 = 10$$
a.. $$100 \div 5 = 20$$

72 is <u>between</u> 50 and 100. So by doing the <u>easy sums</u> 50 ÷ 5 and 100 ÷ 5,
we can <u>work out</u> that 72 ÷ 5 is going to be somewhere between <u>10 and 20</u>.

Split Up the Big number to make it Simpler

We can split up 72 into 50 + 22. So, we can split up the sum into 50 ÷ 5 + 22 ÷ 5.

$$72 \div 5 =$$ $$50 \div 5 = 10$$ Add these two together
                                      to get your answer.
                 $$+$$
$$22 \div 5 = 4 \text{ remainder } 2$$
$$72 \div 5 = 14 \text{ remainder } 2.$$

Now you try some. First estimate the answer then split the big number and work it out.

92 ÷ 7 is between __*140 ÷ 7 = 20*__ and __*70 ÷ 7 = 10*__

92 ÷ 7 = __*70 ÷ 7 = 10* + 22 ÷ 7 = 3 rem 1. *92 ÷ 7 = 13 rem 1*__

65 ÷ 8 is between .... and ....

65 ÷ 8 = ...

83 ÷ 4 is between .... and ....

83 ÷ 4 = ...

61 ÷ 3 is between .... and ....

61 ÷ 3 = ...

77 ÷ 9 is between .... and ....

77 ÷ 9 = ...

When to use × and ÷

When to use _Multiplication_ or _Division_

When a question has "divide", "share", or "how many does each child get", then it's a division question.

When a question has "multiply" or "times" in it then it's a multiplication question.

Sometimes it's not as easy as this to tell:

> I have 24 jelly beans in a bag. My friend John has half as many as me. How many does John have?

This may not look like it, but it's a division question. If John has half as many beans as me, then he has half of **24**, or **12** beans.

Now try some yourself:

> James has some 6-legged beetles.
> How many legs are there on 5 of his beetles?

....

> He also has some 8-legged spiders.
> How many legs are on 10 of his spiders?

....

Rachel eats 5 carrots a day. How many carrots does she eat in 12 days?

....

If there are 25 carrots in the fridge, how many days will it take Rachel to eat them all?

....

15 pairs of socks cost £12.00. How much does one pair cost?

....

Jungo's Marshmallows cost £1.00 for a packet of 50. How much is one mallow?

....

> It takes Freddy the frog 3 weeks to catch a dragonfly. How long does it take him to catch 5 dragonflies?

For a question like this, you'll need to convert between pounds and pence to work it out.

....

> How many does he catch in 24 weeks?

....

When to use × and ÷

If you have 25 pencils, how many people can have five of your pencils each?

....

To make raspberry squash, I need 1 pint of squash for every 5 pints of water.
If I were using 4 pints of squash, how many pints of water would I need?

....

Paul has spent £3 on a Far Paws action figure.
How much would 12 Far Paws figures cost?

....

If Paul had £45 to spend, how many Far Paws
figures would he be able to buy?

....

Matt has 57 hats. If he decides to throw out a third of the hats because
they have too many holes in them, then how many does he have left?

....

If he now throws out half of the
remaining hats, how many does he
have left?

> If a question has several steps in it, do
> one step at a time and take it slowly.
> Work out the first bit, then move on to
> the second part.

....

I have a bag of 75 jelly crocodiles. One third of them are lime flavour and the rest
are lemon flavour. How many lemon flavoured jelly crocodiles have I got?

....

Teresa has 36 scrunchies. She loses a quarter of them. How many does she have left?

....

I bought a sprout sandwich for £1.50. How much would 12 cost?

....

Trevor has a collection of 35 tadpoles. If a fifth
of them die, how many does he have left?

....

Checking Multiplication

Check Your Multiplication by Reversing it

When you are doing a multiplication, and you need to <u>check</u> the <u>answer</u>, then you can <u>reverse</u> the <u>order</u> of the multiplication and work it out <u>again</u>.

EXAMPLE: Work out $2 \times 4 \times 6$.

$2 \times 4 = 8$, $8 \times 6 = 48$. You can check this by:
Work out $6 \times 4 \times 2$: $6 \times 4 = 24$, $24 \times 2 = 48$.

Just remember this simple rule:

It doesn't matter what order the numbers go in.

— the answer should still be the same.

Work out these sums, then check them by reversing them.

$5 \times 2 \times 10 =$ .... = ... $\times$ .... $\times$ ....

$6 \times 1 \times 5 =$ .... = ... $\times$ .... $\times$ ....

$3 \times 4 \times 7 =$ .... = ... $\times$ .... $\times$ ....

$10 \times 3 \times 5 =$ .... = ... $\times$ .... $\times$ ....

$6 \times 4 \times 8 =$ .... = ... $\times$ .... $\times$ ....

$3 \times 7 \times 10 =$ .... = ... $\times$ .... $\times$ ....

Warren has 3 plates with cup cakes on.
There are 12 cup cakes per plate and each
cupcake has 4 hammers on top.
How many hammers are there altogether?

....

= .... $\times$ .... $\times$ ....

Work out these sums, then check them by reversing them.

$12 \times 3 \times 5 =$ .... = ... $\times$ .... $\times$ ....

$7 \times 9 \times 11 =$ .... = ... $\times$ .... $\times$ ....

Check Multiplication and Division

Use Easy sums to check a Multiplication

There are other ways to check a multiplication:

EXAMPLE: Work out $2 \times 4 \times 6$.

You know that $2 \times 4 = 8$, so to check this multiplication you'd work out 8×6.

When you do this, make sure you pick the <u>easiest</u> multiplication to start with. It should be one that you already know off by heart.

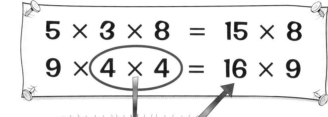

$$5 \times 3 \times 8 = 15 \times 8$$
$$9 \times 4 \times 4 = 16 \times 9$$

This is the easiest sum, so start with it.

Try these for size:

$6 \times 8 \times 10 =$ ......*480*...... = ...*6*...... $\times$ ......*80*......

$5 \times 3 \times 9 =$ .... = ... $\times$ ....

$4 \times 12 \times 2 =$ .... = ... $\times$ ....

$2 \times 6 \times 11 =$ .... = ... $\times$ ....

$8 \times 9 \times 5 =$ .... = ... $\times$ ....

Check jumpers, check trousers... Checking is cool.

Check when you Divide by a Number Ending in 0

What is $800 \div 4$? You know what $80 \div 4$ is, so you can put $(80 \div 4) \times 10$ instead. Now you've got $20 \times 10 = 200$. Checking like this is easy.

Dividing by numbers with a 0 on the end can be easy: Take the 0 off the end of the number, do the sum and then multiply the final answer by 10.

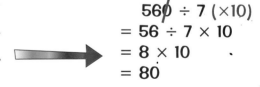

$560 \div 7 \ (\times 10)$
$= 56 \div 7 \times 10$
$= 8 \times 10$
$= 80$

Answer these questions and then check them with another division.

$300 \div 6 =$ ......*50*...... = ...*30*...... $\div$ ......*6*......

$700 \div 7 =$ .... = ... $\div$ ....

$330 \div 3 =$ .... = ... $\div$ ....

$450 \div 15 =$ .... = ... $\div$ ....

$720 \div 8 =$ .... = ... $\div$ ....

You should be able to zip through this lot.

Basic Fractions

Fractions are Parts of a Whole Thing

You need to be able to recognise all the main fractions and know their names.

$\frac{1}{2}$ in words is "one half". Here's half a circle:

$\frac{1}{5}$ in words is "one fifth". Here's one fifth of a circle:

$\frac{1}{20}$ in words is "one twentieth". One twentieth of this shape is shaded in:

Write down these numbers in fraction form:

One tenth .... One sixth ....

One eighth .... One twentieth ....

Write down these fractions in word form:

$\frac{1}{2}$ .... $\frac{1}{3}$ ....

$\frac{1}{10}$ .... $\frac{1}{5}$ ....

What fraction of Carleen's face is covered in chocolate?

....

....

Write down these fractions as words:

$3\frac{1}{2}$ .... $4\frac{1}{3}$ ....

$5\frac{7}{10}$ .... $7\frac{11}{20}$ ....

$4\frac{3}{4}$ *Four and three quarters* .... $5\frac{4}{5}$ ....

Don't forget the units at the front.

Equivalent Fractions

One Half is the same as Two Quarters

Some fractions are worth the same as other fractions: $\frac{3}{6} = \frac{4}{8} = \frac{1}{2}$

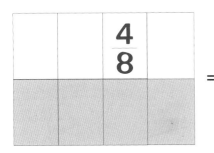

It's a half whichever way you look at it.

For each of these fractions, write down another one that's worth the same.

$\frac{4}{8}$ = ... $\frac{3}{6}$ = ... $\frac{4}{10}$ = ...

$\frac{3}{12}$ = ... $\frac{6}{8}$ = ... $\frac{4}{6}$ = ...

$\frac{8}{10}$ = ... $\frac{2}{3}$ = ... $\frac{1}{2}$ = ...

Are these fractions the same?

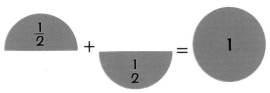   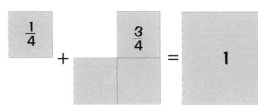

....

....

Adding Fractions to make Whole Numbers

Some fractions add up to make whole numbers: $\frac{1}{2} + \frac{1}{2} = 1$

 +  = 1    +  = 1

Answer these, and see if they add up to whole numbers.

$\frac{1}{2} + \frac{1}{2}$ = ... $1\frac{3}{4} + 2\frac{1}{4}$ = ...

$\frac{3}{8} + \frac{5}{8}$ = ... $\frac{3}{12} + 1\frac{9}{12}$ = ...

$\frac{2}{5} + 3\frac{3}{5}$ = ... $2\frac{1}{6} + 3\frac{5}{6}$ = ...

Ordering Fractions

Putting Fractions in order of size

It's important to know which fractions are <u>bigger</u> than other fractions.
You really need to know which fractions are <u>bigger</u> than a <u>half</u> and which are <u>smaller</u>.

Which of these are bigger than a half? $\frac{3}{4}$, $\frac{1}{6}$, $\frac{3}{10}$, $\frac{1}{4}$, $\frac{3}{8}$.

....

Which of these fractions is bigger than $\frac{1}{4}$? $\frac{1}{8}$, $\frac{1}{3}$, $\frac{3}{10}$, $\frac{1}{5}$, $\frac{3}{4}$, $\frac{1}{6}$

....

Putting Fractions on a number line

<u>Fractions</u> can go on a <u>number line</u> as easily as whole numbers.
You can put marks for <u>halves</u>, <u>quarters</u> and <u>eighths</u> on a number line.

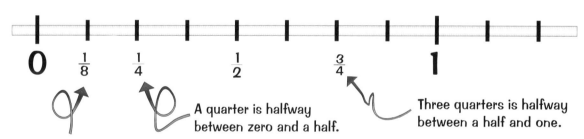

A quarter is halfway
between zero and a half.

Three quarters is halfway
between a half and one.

An eighth is halfway between
zero and a quarter.

Place these fractions on the number line below: $\frac{3}{4}$, $\frac{1}{2}$, 2 , $\frac{1}{4}$, $1\frac{1}{4}$, $1\frac{3}{4}$

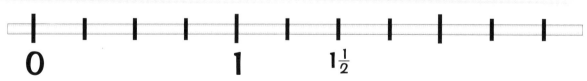

This one's a bit more tricky...

Place these fractions on the number line below: $\frac{2}{3}$, 2 , $1\frac{1}{3}$

Ordering Fractions? — two size $9\frac{1}{2}$ s please...

You'll be all right if you remember which fractions are <u>halfway between</u> which other ones.
And you've really <u>got to know</u> which fractions are <u>bigger or smaller than a half</u> — you've got to.

Division and Fractions

A half of is the same as ÷ 2

Having a half of something is the same as dividing it by 2.

If you have 20 sweets and divide them between 2 people, each person gets 10 sweets.

=

If you have 20 sweets and you split them in half, you get 10 sweets.

Is 56 ÷ 2 equal to a half of 56? ....

Is 24 ÷ 4 equal to a half of 24? ....

Fractions mean Division

Dividing something by 3 is the same as having a third of it, and having a quarter of something is the same as dividing it by 4.

EXAMPLE: Sarah has 20 false nails and wants to share them between 4 friends. What fraction will each person get?

If she divides them between 4 people, each of them will get a quarter.

If I share 60 Malt Wheezers between 5 people, what fraction does each person get?

....

What is a tenth of 120?

....

To find a third of 75 what do I have to divide by?

....

What is an eighth of 48?

....

I have 91 pencil-eating alarm clocks, and I want to find a seventh of the collection. What do I have to divide by to find a seventh, and what is a seventh of 91?

....

....

....

Decimals

Place Value in Decimals

Decimals are another way to show numbers that are smaller than 1. A decimal point is a dot that goes after the units. The digits after the point are all smaller than 1.

The names of the digits that come after the decimal point end in "th". Tenths come first, then hundredths.

Tens Units Tenths Hundredths

12.57

These digits have a place value smaller than 1.

Decimal point

What is the value of the tenths digit in these numbers?

1.23 *2 tenths* ....   2.79 ....   4.83 ....

12.99 ....   9.35 ....   3.05 ....

What is the value of the hundredths digit in these numbers?

1.23 *3 hundredths* ....   4.76 ....   8.91 ....

34.07 ....   1.12 ....   4.801 ....

How much is a tenth of a metre in cm? ....

How much is a hundredth of a pound in pence? ....

Decimals are in Money and Measurements

You write "three pounds and fifty pence" as £3.50.
The dot between the pounds and the pence is a decimal point.

Write these measurements in decimals:

450 pence in pounds ....   350 cm in metres ....

5600 ml in litres ....   420 cm in metres ....

Don't forget how many centimetres there are in a metre and how many millilitres there are in a litre.

Write 1.35 m in metres and centimetres. ....

Write 2.52 ml in litres and millilitres. ....

Fletcher has a 2.36 cm long hair on his nose. What is this in cm and mm?

....

Counting in Decimals

Count in Decimals

When you're counting down, the hardest bit is that first step going down from 1 to 0.9.

0   0.1   0.2   0.3   0.4   0.5   0.6   0.7   0.8   0.9   1

+0.1   +0.1

Counting up in 0.1s is like counting in 1s, except there's a 0 and a decimal point at the front.

Answer these simple sums:

$0 + 0.1 =$ ....

$0 + 0.1 + 0.1 =$ ....

$0.5 + 0.1 =$ ....

$0.3 + 0.1 + 0.1 + 0.1 =$ ....

$0.9 + 0.1 =$ ....

$0.9 + 0.1 + 0.1 =$ ....

And here's some more of them:

$2.3 - 0.1 =$ ....

$5 - 0.1 - 0.1 =$ ....

$5.4 - 0.1 =$ ....

$6.9 - 0.1 - 0.1 - 0.1 =$ ....

$3.7 - 0.1 =$ ....

$4.2 - 0.1 - 0.1 =$ ....

$2.5 - 0.1 =$ ....

$3.5 - 0.1 + 0.1 - 0.1 =$ ....

Decimals on Number lines

You can use number lines to help with decimals as well.

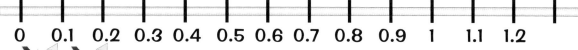

0   0.1   0.2 0.3 0.4   0.5 0.6 0.7   0.8   0.9   1   1.1   1.2

+0.1   +0.1

Each step on this number line means going up or down by 0.1.

Label 0.1, 0.6, 0.3, 0.7 and 1.3 on the number line below.

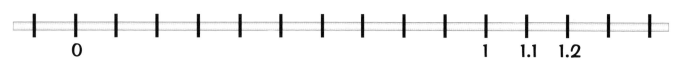

0   1   1.1   1.2

Label the marked decimals on the number line below.

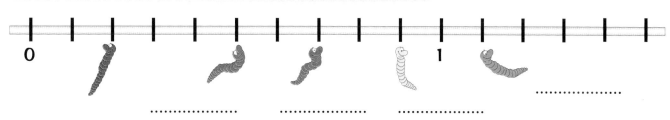

0   1

                                                          ....

....

Understanding Effect of Addition

Add Two Positive Numbers to get a Bigger One

Danny the Dinosaur is very proud of his CD collection. He already has 68 CDs, and he buys another 24 from his friend Stegosaurus Sam. How many CDs does he have now?

$$68 + 24 = \text{..........} \text{ CDs}$$

Have a look at your <u>answer</u>. Notice that it's <u>bigger</u> than 68 and <u>bigger</u> than 24.

It's pretty <u>obvious</u> really — if you add 24 CDs to 68 CDs you're going to get a number of CDs that's bigger than 24 and bigger than 68. This is a <u>rule</u> — the sum of <u>two positive numbers</u> is always <u>bigger</u> than either number.

Add these numbers and check that the answer is bigger than either number.

35 + 61 = *96* , which is *bigger* than 35 or 61.

103 + 42 = ..., which is .... than 103 or 42.

97 + 18 = ..., which is .... than 97 or 18.

145 + 30 = ..., which is .... than 145 or 30.

58 + 46 = ..., which is .... than 58 or 46.

Adding Nothing leaves the Number Unchanged

Here's one that's even more <u>obvious</u>. If Danny has 68 CDs and he <u>doesn't</u> buy any more, how many does he have? Yes, it's that <u>easy</u> — 68.

This is <u>another</u> rule — adding <u>0</u> to a number leaves you with the <u>same</u> number that you <u>started</u> with.

Check for yourself by doing these sums.

75 + 0 = *75*   132 + 0 = ...

0 + 97 = ...   415 + 0 = ...

49 + 0 = ...   0 + 101 = ...

+ and – by Counting in Steps

Do Sums by Counting in 10s, 100s or 1000s

Here's a sum that looks pretty <u>scary</u> — but I'll show you an <u>easy</u> way to do it. ⟶ **5229 + 40**

5229   **5239**   **5249**   **5259**   **5269**

Ten   Twenty   Thirty   Forty

It's easy to count up in <u>steps of 10</u>, so do that until you've added <u>40</u>.

Count up or down in 10s, 100s or 1000s to do these sums.

$9823 - 500 =$ ..9723.. , ..9623.. , ..9523.. , ..9423.. , (..9323..).

$3692 + 3000 =$ ...., ..., (..........).

$5781 - 60 =$ ...., ..., ..., ..., ..., (..........).

Do these in your <u>head</u>.

$4711 - 200 =$ ....

$4124 + 400 =$ ....

$1323 + 70 =$ ....

$8773 - 7000 =$ ....

You can use this method to <u>add</u> numbers that are <u>nearly</u> a multiple of 10, 100 or 1000.

5229 + 39 ⟶ Easy — do <u>5229 + 40</u>, then <u>take away 1</u>.

Count up or down in 10s, 100s or 1000s then adjust to do these sums.

$5229 + 39 =$ $5229 + 40 - 1$ = $5269 - 1$ = 5268 .

$4867 - 498 =$ .... = ... = ...

$3213 + 701 =$ .... = ... = ...

$8578 - 5003 =$ .... = ... = ...

$6439 + 58 =$ .... = ... = ...

Adding by Compensating

Add Too Much then Take Away — it's easy

Albert the Adder is off on his holidays.
He's already slithered 435 miles from home,
and he's got another 87 to go.

How far will he have travelled in total, when he gets there?

87 is 13 less than 100.
So, here's an easy way to do the sum:

$$\begin{array}{r} 4\ 3\ 5 \\ +\ 8\ 7 \\ \hline \end{array}$$

First, add 100... ⟶ 535

$$-\ 1\ 3$$

... then take away the 13. ⟶ 522

Work out these sums by adding too much then taking away.

$$\begin{array}{r} 3\ 2\ 7 \\ +\ 9\ 6 \\ \hline 4\ 2\ 7 \\ -\quad\ 4 \\ \hline 4\ 2\ 3 \\ \dotfill \end{array}$$

I grew them myself.

$$\begin{array}{r} 5\ 7\ 8 \\ +\ 8\ 8 \\ \hline \end{array}$$
....

...so I'm taking some back.

$$\begin{array}{r} 6\ 1\ 1 \\ +\ 9\ 8 \\ \hline \end{array}$$
....

$$\begin{array}{r} 8\ 9\ 7 \\ +\ 9\ 1 \\ \hline \end{array}$$
....

$$\begin{array}{r} 7\ 5\ 6 \\ +\ 8\ 5 \\ \hline \end{array}$$
....

$$\begin{array}{r} 2\ 4\ 4 \\ +\ 9\ 4 \\ \hline \end{array}$$
....

$$\begin{array}{r} 3\ 9\ 4 \\ +\ 8\ 6 \\ \hline \end{array}$$
....

$$\begin{array}{r} 4\ 0\ 4 \\ +\ 9\ 9 \\ \hline \end{array}$$
....

I've ADD TOO MUCH of this...

If one number is near a multiple of 10, 100 or 1000, you can make the sum easier by adding or taking away the big, round number first, then adjusting it to get the answer.

Time Conversions

1 Hour equals 60 Minutes

How many seconds in:

20 minutes? .... 1 hour? ....

How many minutes in:

1.5 hours? .... 7 hours? ....

How many hours in:

5 days? .... 7 days? ....

1 minute = 60 seconds

1 hour = 60 minutes

1 day = 24 hours

1 Century equals 100 Years

1 year = 365 days

1 year = 52 weeks

1 year = 12 months

1 month = 4 weeks

1 week = 7 days

1 century = 100 years

1 millennium = 1000 years

How many years in:

730 days? .... 52 weeks? ....

36 months .... 78 weeks? ....

3 centuries? .... 2 millennia? ....

How many months in:

6 years? .... 52 weeks? ....

How many days in:

5 years? .... 12 weeks? ....

There can be 28, 29, 30 or 31 Days in a Month

The best way to remember them is to learn this rhyme. Then read it out loud each time you need to know how many days are in a certain month.

"30 days has September,

April, June and November.

All the rest have 31,

Except February alone.

Which has 28 days clear.

And 29 in each leap year."

Analogue and Digital Clocks

Reading Digital Clocks

The <u>first digit</u> is the number of <u>hours</u>. Here, it's <u>6</u>.  **6:48** The <u>second two digits</u> are the number of <u>minutes</u> <u>past the hour</u>. Here, it's <u>48 minutes past</u>.

The time is <u>6.48</u> or <u>48 minutes past 6</u> or <u>12 minutes to 7</u>.

What is the time, in words, on these clocks?

3:03

3 minutes past 3

4:58

....

12:25

....

5:55

....

1:17

....

2:43

....

9:50

....

3:32

....

....

Reading Analogue Clocks

The <u>little hand</u> is the number of <u>hours</u>. Here, it's <u>4</u>.

The <u>big hand</u> is the number of <u>minutes past the hour</u>. Here, it's <u>5</u> minutes past.

This will take <u>5 minutes</u> for the <u>minute hand</u> and <u>1 hour</u> for the <u>hour hand</u>.

The time is <u>five past four</u>, or <u>4:05</u>.

What are the times on these clocks?

....

....

....

And these watches...?

....

....

....

....

....

More Time Problems

Hands or numbers — both tell the same time

 =  = 43 minutes past 2
or 17 minutes to 3

EXAMPLE Write 20 minutes to 4 as a digital time.

 Change it to the right hour.
If it's "... past," you keep it the same.
For "... to," you take away 1.

$4 - 1 = 3$ hours

 Change it to minutes past the hour.
If it's already "... past", leave it like that.
If it's "... minutes to," take away the minutes from 60.

$60 - 20$

$= 40$ minutes

So, the time is 40 minutes past 3. And in digital, that's

Put these times in digital form.

twenty past four ....

12 minutes to 12 ....

half past five ....

five to 6 ....

five past eleven ....

thirteen minutes to 3 ....

AM means Morning and PM means Afternoon

"am" means "Morning" — or 12 midnight to 12 noon.
"pm" means "Afternoon and Evening" — or 12 noon to 12 midnight.

The main thing to remember is that Midnight is 12:00 am and Midday is 12:00 pm.

Write these times down in digital form, adding am or pm:

20 past 5 in the morning ....

5:30 in the evening ....

10 past 10 in the evening ....

2:40 in the afternoon ....

12:10 at night ....

12:15 in the afternoon ....

Handling Data	**_Tally Charts_**

A <u>tally chart</u> is the best way to <u>start</u>. Hey, that rhymes...

One Dash means One Vote

You've all seen tally charts before — dead easy.

<u>Just the other day</u>, someone asked me:

Which flavour of Froggatt's Instant Lumpy Soup is most popular?

... so I thought I'd <u>find out</u>.

I asked <u>30 teachers</u> their favourite flavour, and put the results in a <u>tally chart</u>.
The flavour with the <u>most dashes</u> is the <u>most popular</u>.

Soup Flavour	Tally
	III
	IIII IIII
	II
	IIII IIII
	IIII
	I

Look — the most popular
flavour is Lobster and Vinegar.
It's got 10 votes.

Save the
Basking Shark

Which flavour was the least popular?

How many voted for Honey and Turnip?

....

....

Right — your turn. Try this on your friends...

Ask 20 people which of these sports they
prefer. Fill in this tally chart as you go.

Don't forget — every
fifth one goes through
the other four.

Which is the most popular sport?

....

How many people's favourite sport was cycling?

....

Which was the least popular? ....

Can you think of a way of making this a better questionnaire?

....

Favourite Sport	Tally
Running	
Football	
Rollerblading	
Rounders	
Swimming	
Cycling	

I love TALLY CHARTS — I'm a TALLY ADDICT...

Whenever you need to count the number of votes, mark them straight into a <u>tally chart</u>.
They're always grouped in fives, so they're easy to count up afterwards.

Frequency Tables

OK, so you thought tally charts were good — well, how about frequency tables, then...

One Tally Mark means a Frequency of 1

The frequency is just how many there are. Count up the marks in the tally chart, and put the number in the frequency chart. Dead easy.

Use the tally chart below to finish off the frequency chart.

Favourite Perfume	Tally
Cabbage	JHH
Sprout Spray	JHH II
Country Air	I
Toilet Water	III
Smell Number 5	JHH
Mouldy Spice	IIII

Favourite Perfume	Frequency
Cabbage	5
Sprout Spray	7
Country Air	
Toilet Water	
Smell Number 5	
Mouldy Spice	

Which perfume is the most popular?

....

Which is the least popular?

....

This tally chart shows people's favourite clothes to wear to parties.
(I asked 30 of my relatives.) Fill in the frequency column.

Favourite Clothes	Tally	Frequency
Clown Outfit	JHH III	
Suit of Armour	JHH	
Ball Gown	JHH IIII	
Grubby Overalls	II	
Elephant Ears	IIII	
Yellow Dungarees	II	

Remember — count up the marks in the tally column.

I asked 30 people what their favourite animal was. These were the answers:

tiger, dog, cat, hamster, cat, dog, cat, dog, dog, tiger, cat, tiger, dog, dog, tiger, dog, tiger, cat, dog, dog, cat, tiger, cat, hamster, cat, dog, tiger, cat, cat, dog

Make a tally first, then work out the frequency. (Write them in this table.)

	Tally	Frequency

Handling Data	# Reading Bar Charts

The Height of each Bar shows the Frequency

You need to understand all the bits of a bar chart.

You read across from the bar to find the number of people on each shuttle.

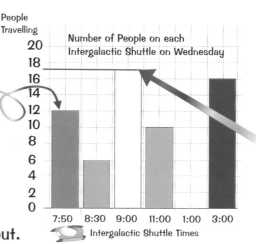

People Travelling — Number of People on each Intergalactic Shuttle on Wednesday

There were 12 people on the 7:50 shuttle.

This bar is between 16 and 18. Drawing a line shows it's halfway between them, so the value is 17.

The labels tell you what the chart is about.

Intergalactic Shuttle Times

How many people were on the 7:50 shuttle? ....

Which shuttle had the most people on? ....

Which shuttle had the fewest people on? ....

Look at the bar chart on the right and answer these questions on it:

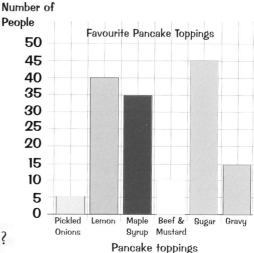

Number of People — Favourite Pancake Toppings

Pancake toppings

What was the favourite pancake topping?

....

What was the least favourite pancake topping?

....

How many people's favourite topping was lemon?

....

How many people's favourite topping was beef and mustard?

....

How many more votes did maple syrup get than pickled onions?

....

Drawing Bar Charts

Bar charts are a real doddle to draw. As long as you're careful, that is.

Use a Ruler to find the Top of the Bar

This frequency chart shows the different animals I found in my garden last week.
I've started putting the results into a bar chart.

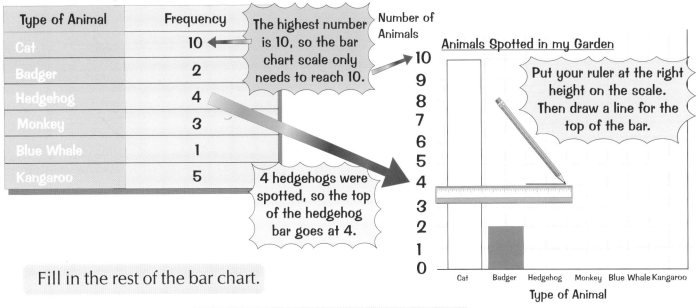

Type of Animal	Frequency
Cat	10
Badger	2
Hedgehog	4
Monkey	3
Blue Whale	1
Kangaroo	5

The highest number is 10, so the bar chart scale only needs to reach 10.

Number of Animals

Animals Spotted in my Garden

Put your ruler at the right height on the scale. Then draw a line for the top of the bar.

4 hedgehogs were spotted, so the top of the hedgehog bar goes at 4.

Type of Animal

Fill in the rest of the bar chart.

Which animal did I find fewest of?

....

This is a table showing 30 people's favourite octopus names.
Draw a bar chart of the results on the squared paper below.

Favourite Name	Frequency
Ollie	15
Orrid	6
Oscar	8
Obi	4
Offul	5
Orvil	2

Work out the right scale for the bar chart first.

What is the most popular name?

....

What is the least popular name?

....

How many votes did Orvil get?

....

Numbers and the Number System	# Counting in 10s, 100s and 1000s

You only *Change One Digit*

When you count in hundreds, you don't need to change the tens or units digits.
I'm counting up 500 (in hundreds) from 1380, so the only digit I'll change is the 3...

1380   **1480**   **1580**   **1680**   **1780**   **1880**

+ 100   + 100   + 100   + 100   + 100

Count up 40 in tens from 1560.

1560, 1570, 1580, 1590, 1600

Count up 300 from 245 in hundreds.

....

Count up 3000 in thousands from 2130.

Count up 5000 from 4056 in thousands.

....

Counting down means take away, and counting up means add on.

Count down 30 from 246, in tens.

....

Count down 200 from 902, in hundreds.

Count down 600 from 2889, in hundreds.

....

Count down 4000 from 7320, in thousands.

....

Don't let this next lot catch you out...
they're just the same, really.

What is 10p more than £3.56?

What is 10 cm less than 1 m?

....

What is 100 g more than 568 g?

....

Darren was 167 cm tall. He has just shrunk by 100 cm.
How tall is he now?

....

Darren has already had a 356 kg rock dropped on his head.
He is just about to have another 100 kg dropped on him.
How many kilograms will have been dropped on him, in total?

....

Multiplying and Dividing by 10

Move the Digits to the Left to Multiply by 10

EXAMPLE: What is 35 × 10?

Th H T U

3 5

So what's 35 × 100?

3 5 0 ← The easy way is...
...stick a 0 on the end.

Just multiply by 10 again...

3 5 0 0 ← ...and stick another 0 on the end.

Do these multiplications by moving the digits, like I've just done.

23 × 10 = ...   23 × 10 × 10 = ...   23 × 10 × 10 × 10 = ...

57 × 10 = ...   57 × 10 × 10 = ...   57 × 10 × 10 × 10 = ...

63 × 10 = ...   63 × 10 × 10 = ...   57 × 10 × 10 × 10 = ...

 Multiplying by 100 is the same as × 10 × 10.
Keep on going as normal, put <u>two zeros</u> on the end, and move everything <u>two places to the left</u>.

49 × 100 = ...   150 × 100 = ...   1302 × 100 = ...

72 × 1000 = ...   6722 × 1000 = ...

Move the Digits to the Right to Divide by 10

EXAMPLE: What is 4700 ÷ 10?

Th H T U

4 7 0 0 → The easy way is...
...drop a 0 from the end.

Divide by 10 again...

So what's 4700 ÷ 100?

4 7 0 → ...and drop another 0.

4 7

 No, you can't relax just yet...

Have a go at these divisions:

110 ÷ 10 = ...   1200 ÷ 10 ÷ 10 = ...

150 ÷ 10 = ...   4320 ÷ 10 = ...

4350 ÷ 10 = ...   2900 ÷ 10 ÷ 10 = ...

42000 ÷ 10 ÷ 10 = ...   42000 ÷ 10 ÷ 10 ÷ 10 = ...

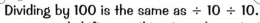 Dividing by 100 is the same as ÷ 10 ÷ 10.
Drop <u>two zeros</u> and shift everything <u>two places to the right</u>.

3700 ÷ 100 = ...

2500 ÷ 100 = ...

Negative Numbers

A Negative Number has – at the front

If you see a number like –4 then it's a negative number.
–249, –898, –2, –3, –56 are all negative numbers.

Look at this number ladder.

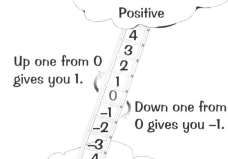

Positive

Up one from 0 gives you 1.

Down one from 0 gives you –1.

Negative

┌───┐
│ If you go <u>up a rung</u>, you <u>add 1</u>.   │
│ If you go <u>down a rung</u>, you <u>subtract 1</u>. │
└───┘

Using the number ladder, work out these sums:

$4 - 1 =$ .... $0 - 1 =$ ....

$2 - 4 =$ .... $1 - 3 =$ .... $4 - 8 =$ ....

$3 - 7 =$ .... $1 - 1 =$ .... $2 - 8 =$ ....

Label these positive and negative points on the number line:

-10   ↑   ↑   ↑   **0**   ↑   ↑   **10**

....

Reginald got all confused at the start of the Garden Pond Number Line Race and jumped 8 lilypads backwards.

You could say he was –8 ...... lilypads from the start.

-10   -8   **0**   **10**

1 backwards from 0 on a number line gives -1.   1 Forward from 0 on a number line gives 1.

Reginald is now at the <u>5th</u> lilypad. Which lilypad would he land on if he hopped:

3 hops to the left? ....

or   8 hops to the left? ....

or   12 hops to the left? ....

or   6 hops to the left? ....

Negative Numbers

Negative Temperatures are very Cold

Thermometers are like number lines or rulers.
You read them the same, too.

This thermometer reads –5 °C.
Brrrrrr...

-20 -15 -10 -5   0   5   10   15   20 25   30   °C

The scale is the same as a number line — each mark is equal to 1 °C.

What are the readings on these thermometers?

................°C

-20 -15 -10 -5   0   5   10   °C

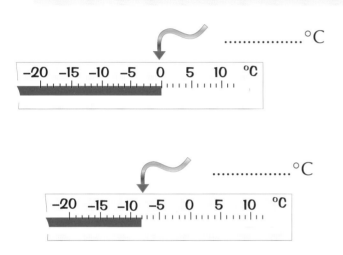

................°C

-20 -15 -10 -5   0   5   10   °C

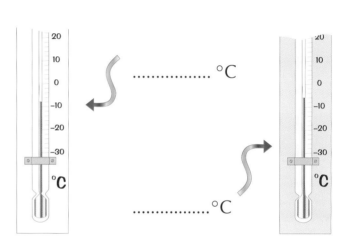

................°C

................°C

Negative numbers can also be ordered

EXAMPLE: Theo is sick, and his fire has gone out.
I measured Theo's temperature for 7 days.

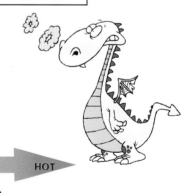

Day	Mon	Tue	Wed	Thu	Fri	Sat	Sun
Temperature (°C)	99	50	-15	0	100	-20	-7

Put them in <u>order</u> of coldest to hottest   COLD ➜ HOT

1. Order the positive numbers separately   0, 50, 99, 100
2. Order the negative numbers   -20, -15, -7
3. Put it all together   -20, -15, -7, 0, 50, 99, 100

NEGATIVE ➜ POSITIVE

Order these sets of numbers, smallest first.

12, 34, 4, 0, 24, 67, 5, 10 ....

32, 6, 0, 2, 4, -4, 6, 46 ....

26, 12, -12, -3, -45, 9, 25 ....

Measuring, Shape and Space

Reading Real Life Scales

Read Measuring Jug Scales at Eye-Level

Reading from scales is nearly as easy as reading from thermometers and rulers — just make sure your eye is at the same level as the liquid, or you'll get it wrong.

How much juice is there in Arnold's big glass of Jupiter Juice?

This one's easy. Look where the level of juice is up to on the scale. It's up to the 750 ml mark. So there is 750 ml of Jupiter Juice.

Arnold

Read the scales on the following equipment. Don't forget the units.

....

....

....

....

Urghh — cold tea...

The 3 Rules of Measuring
1) Always put it on a flat surface.
2) Read the scale at eye-level.
3) Don't knock anything!

My aunt likes to weigh her feet every morning. How much do her feet weigh today?

....

How much does this scary ghost weigh?

....

How much swamp water is there in the measuring jug?

....

Understanding Subtraction

When you **Subtract**, you get a **Smaller Number**

96 children are taking part in a <u>rally</u> against <u>homework</u>.
23 of them are rounded up by the Police and
told to get back to school.
<u>How many</u> children are left?

$$96 - 23 = \dots\dots\dots$$

If you've done the sum <u>right</u>, your
answer should be <u>less than 96</u>.

It's obvious, really. When you <u>take away</u> a positive number, you've got <u>less left</u>.

Do these subtraction sums and check that the answer is a smaller number.

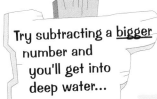

$77 - 36 = \dots\dots\dots$ $19 - 13 = \dots\dots\dots$ Try subtracting a <u>bigger</u> number and you'll get into deep water... $4 - 5 = \dots\dots\dots$ EEEEK

$98 - 18 = \dots\dots\dots$ $110 - 105 = \dots\dots\dots$ $10 - 20 = \dots\dots\dots$ EEEEK

$137 - 51 = \dots\dots\dots$ $1000 - 1 = \dots\dots\dots$

$100 - 24 = \dots\dots\dots$ $246 - 46 = \dots\dots\dots$

Subtracting 0 leaves the Number **The Same**

You know <u>adding 0</u> leaves the number <u>the same</u>... well, so does <u>taking away 0</u>.

It's <u>easy</u> to remember — if you've got six bears and you take <u>none</u> of them away...

... you've <u>still</u> got six bears.

Do these sums and you'll see what I mean:

$6 - 0 = \dots\dots\dots$ $147 - 0 = \dots\dots\dots$ $22 - 0 = \dots\dots\dots$

$45 - 0 = \dots\dots\dots$ $96 - 0 = \dots\dots\dots$ $305 - 0 = \dots\dots\dots$

Calculations | **Addition and Subtraction Facts**

Add and Subtract Numbers up to 20

You need to be very <u>familiar</u> with adding and taking away the numbers <u>up to 20</u>, so you can do them in your head without really <u>thinking</u> about it.

Pick out the pairs that add up to 15 — I've done the first pair for you.

9	+ 1 = 15
14	+ 4 = 15
8	+ 6 = 15
2	+ 7 = 15
11	+ 10 = 15
3	+ 12 = 15
5	+ 13 = 15

7 + 8 = 15, baby

Ooh, you're dead clever.

No, I didn't mean <u>pears</u>.

Write down what number you need to subtract from 19 to get these answers.

What do you need to <u>add to the</u> <u>answer</u> to <u>get 19</u>?

19 − .... = 7   19 − .... = 11

19 − .... = 2   19 − .... = 5

19 − .... = 15   19 − .... = 13

19 − .... = 18   19 − .... = 10

Fill in the gaps in these sums as quickly as you can.

4 + 7 = ... − 5 = 8   8 + 9 = ...

20 − 12 = ...   2 + 14 = ... − 13 = 4

3 + ... = 13   16 − .... = 5   11 − .... = 3

17 − .... = 12   .... + 7 = 20   .... + 11 = 18

Subtracting by Compensating

Take Away Too Much and Add Some Back

When you're <u>subtracting</u> a number that's <u>just less</u> than a big, round number, it's easier to take away <u>too much</u> first, then <u>add</u> some back.

97 is only <u>3 less</u> than 100.
So we'll <u>start</u> by taking 100
away from 746, <u>then</u> add 3.

First, <u>take away</u> 100... ➜

... then <u>add back</u> the 3.

```
   7 4 6
 -   9 7
 ─────────
   6 4 6
 +     3
 ─────────
   6 4 9
```

Mmm...
too much
take away

Take away too much then add some back to do these sums.

```
   8 5 7          3 8 1          5 2 8
 -   9 6        -   9 5        -   9 2
 ─────────      ─────────      ─────────
   7 5 7
 +     4
 ─────────
   7 6 1
 ............    ............    ............
```

You get the <u>idea</u>
— so here are
some more.

```
   5 1 8          4 2 2
 -   9 9        -   8 9
 ─────────      ─────────



 ─────────      ─────────
 ............    ............
```

```
   2 6 3          8 6 8          6 4 2
 -   8 7        -   9 0        -   8 0
 ─────────      ─────────      ─────────



 ─────────      ─────────      ─────────
 ............    ............    ............
```

Money Problems

Work out what Sum to do, then Do it

Sometimes you'll be given a problem involving <u>money</u>.
You'll have to spot what <u>sum</u> you need to do, then do it.

Tiddles has been <u>shopping</u>. She's going to make her favourite dinner — <u>mashed mango on toast</u>.
The loaf of bread cost 69 pence, and the mangoes cost £2.30. <u>How much</u> did Tiddles spend?

Looks like an <u>addition</u> sum to me — add the cost of the <u>bread</u> to the cost of the <u>mangoes</u>.

£2.30 + 69p = £2.99

Work out these money problems.

Princess Lisa buys a dragon which costs £70.

She also buys a pig to feed it, which costs £22.50.

How much does she spend in total?

The sum you need to do is ....

The answer is ....

Greedy Graham wants the moon on a stick.
He spends £9.25 of his £10 at a wishing well.

How much does he have left?

The sum you need to do is ....

The answer is ....

Aman is hungry. He takes £10 to the supermarket and spends £7.60 on 48 packets of crisps. How much change does he get?

The sum you need to do is .... and the answer is ....

Which Subtractions are Easiest?

Some sums are easy and others are hard. Here are some easy ones:

180 – 100 = ...

250 – 50 = ...

130 – 30 = ...

2500 – 1500 = ...

6000 – 4000 = ...

175 – 5 = ...

333 – 111 = ...

220 – 200 = ...

Decide which ones are the Easiest Sums

Which is the easiest out of these sums?   I'm going to try to do them, and find out...

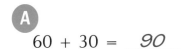 **A**
 60 + 30 = *90*

  B
 68 + 27 = *95*

  C
 55 + 31 = *86*

I reckon <u>sum A</u> was easiest.
I only had to add up the <u>tens</u> bit.

<u>Sums B and C</u> were harder, because
I had to add up the <u>units</u> as well.

 *EASY*

NOT SO EASY

Do these sums and say which you found the easiest. Then say why.

A   **B**   **C**

180 — 137 = ...   180 — 100 = ...   180 — 161 = ...

The easiest sum is .... because ....

....

Do these sums and say which you found the hardest. Then say why.

  A
 301 – 178 = ...

B
 301 – 101 = ...

  C
 301 – 130 = ...

The hardest sum is .... because ....

....

Sum Trouble? — Take the easy way out...

If it looks hard, make it easier. You know lots of tricks, so use them. You can split the numbers into tens and units, or use adding facts you already know... the list is endless.

Measures, Shape and Space

Conversions Between Units

Change Metric Units by Shifting the Digits

To change from one metric unit to another, you always have to multiply or divide by things like 10, 100 or 1000. So all you do is shift the digits, then put in or drop the extra noughts.

The only hard bit is learning the conversions, so I've put them in a big yellow box to help you remember...

OK, cover them up and see if you can answer these:

What is 1 kg in grams?

....

What is 1 l in millilitres?

....

What is 1 km in metres?

....

Remember
10 mm = 1 cm
100 cm = 1 m
1000 m = 1 km
1000 ml = 1 l
1000 g = 1 kg

What is 1 m in centimetres?

....

OK, that's the really easy stuff out of the way...

What's 1000 mm in cm? *1 cm = 10 mm, so there must be 10 times as many mm as cm.*
That means I should divide 1000 mm by 10.
Easy — I'll just knock a 0 off the end. So, 1000 mm = 100 cm.

Go on, you have a go.

Change:

2 l into ml ....

5000 g into kilograms ....

3 km into m ....

2000 m into km ....

500 cm into m ....

0.5 kg into grams ....

100 mm into cm ....

10 cm into mm ....

5 kg into g ....

3000 ml into l ....

Barry has 3 litres of custard in his cheeks.

How many millilitres is this?   ....

John has a 4.5 kg rock on his toe.

How many grams is the rock?   ....

Conversions Between Units

Change it into the Same Units First

EXAMPLE: Write 3 m and 25 cm in just cm.

Firstly convert both measurements into the same unit, then add them together.
Well, 3 m is equal to 300 cm, so 3 m and 25 cm = 325 cm.

You need to know those facts from the last page.

What is 300 g in kg? ....

What is 1400 ml in l? ....

What is 0.35 km in m? ....

What is 0.2 cm in mm? ....

Now for a few harder ones:

What is 10 l and 300 ml in l? ....

What is 3 kg 500 g in kg? ....

What is 30 km and 200 m in m? ....

Mr Greenacre's fence is 1600 cm long. How long is this in m?

....

Keith has a knot in his tongue.
It is 3 cm and 8 mm wide.
How wide is this in mm?

....

....

Sylvester the Clown is 140 cm tall, but wears 1 m stilts.
How tall is he including the stilts?

....

Perimeters

The Perimeter is the Length around All the Sides

The perimeter of a shape is the distance around its edges.
It's what you get if you add up the length of all the sides.

25 mm

EXAMPLE: What is the perimeter of this rectangle?

The rectangle has two sides of
25 mm and two sides of 60 mm.
Check for yourself with a ruler.

60 mm

60 mm

To find the perimeter, add up the
lengths of all the sides:

25 + 25 + 60 + 60 = 170 mm

25 mm

Find the perimeters of these shapes by using a ruler to measure the sides.

Write down the lengths of the sides:

.... + ... + ... + ...

The perimeter is .... mm.

.... + ... + ...

The perimeter is .... mm.

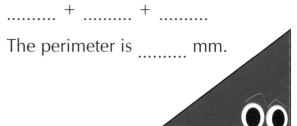

.... + ... + ...

The perimeter is .... mm.

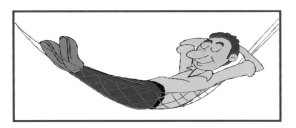

.... + ... + ... + ...

The perimeter is .... mm.

Perimeters

Perimeters of Real Things

Measuring with a ruler is <u>one way</u> to find out the perimeter. But if you're <u>told</u> what the lengths of the sides are, you don't <u>need</u> a ruler — you only need to <u>add them up</u>.

What is the perimeter of this table top?

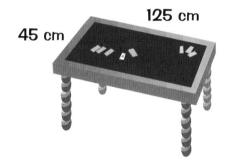

125 cm

45 cm

You're <u>told</u> that the table top measures <u>45</u> cm by <u>125</u> cm.

_125_ .... + _125_ .... + _45_ .... + _45_ .... = ... cm

Work out the perimeters from the information that you're given.

Farmer Jekyll is growing genetically modified strawberry-flavoured turnips in a field that's 750 m long and 1000 m wide. What's the perimeter of the field?

.... + ... + ... + ... = ... m

The groundsman of Bootle AFC is about to paint the perimeter of the football pitch. The pitch measures 45 m by 80 m. How long is the perimeter that he will have to paint?

.... + ... + ... + ... = ... m

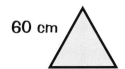

60 cm

An equilateral triangle with sides of 60 cm has a perimeter of .... cm.

90 cm

A square with sides of 90 cm has a perimeter of .... cm.

Measures, Shape and Space	**Symmetry**

Line Symmetry is when a Shape Reflects Itself

If a shape is the same either side of a <u>line of symmetry</u>, it is <u>symmetrical</u>.
It's like one <u>half</u> of the shape is looking at itself in a <u>mirror</u>.

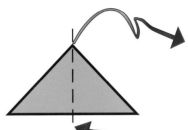

The <u>halves</u> of the triangle either side of this line are <u>the same</u>, but one's been flipped over.

This line is the <u>line of symmetry</u>.

This kind of symmetry is like <u>reflections</u> in a mirror.
The bit on one side is like a <u>reflection</u> of the other.

Hmm... I look very symmetrical today

Do these shapes have any lines of symmetry? If so, draw them on.

(There may be more than one.)

YES ☐   NO ☐

YES ☐   NO ☐

YES ☐   NO ☐

YES ☐   NO ☐

YES ☐   NO ☐

Sketch the rest of these shapes on the other side of the line of symmetry.

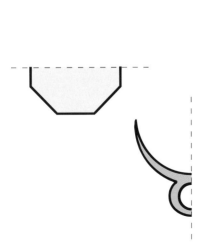

Translations

Translation is when you Move a Shape

Translation is <u>only</u> about <u>moving</u> a shape. If you <u>flip</u> it, <u>turn</u> it, make it <u>bigger</u> or <u>smaller</u> or <u>change</u> its shape — then it <u>isn't</u> a translation.

Which of these are translations?

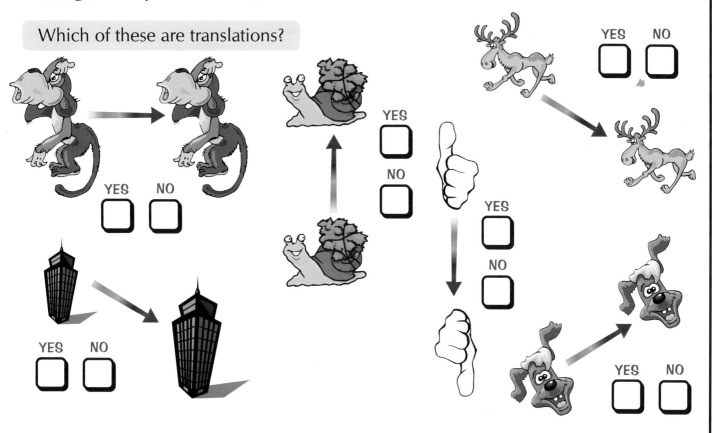

Lots of Translations can make a Pattern

If you translate <u>one shape</u> to lots of <u>different places</u>, you can make <u>patterns</u>!

Make patterns by drawing translations of these shapes along the lines.

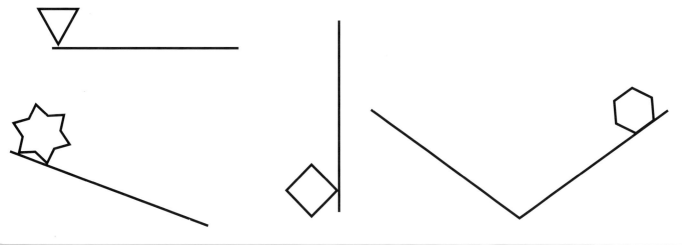

Measures, Shape and Space

Making Shapes

Make 2-D Shapes by Folding and Cutting Paper

It's easy to <u>make</u> shapes by folding or cutting paper.
Get three <u>square</u> sheets of paper and fold or cut them along these <u>dotted</u> lines.

Write down the names of the shapes you get after you've folded or cut the paper.

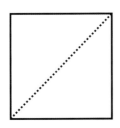

Triangle
....

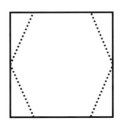

....

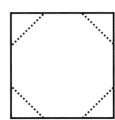

....

Draw Polygons on a Grid or Pegboard

You can also make the <u>outlines</u> of shapes by drawing <u>dots</u> on a grid or putting <u>pegs</u> in a pegboard, like the ones below.

Fill in the missing shape names. You can join the dots up, if it helps.

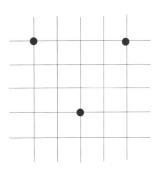

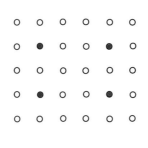

....

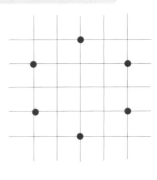

....

....

....

Your turn to make shapes, now.

Start by putting a dot where <u>one corner</u> is going to be. The squares and peg holes are <u>evenly spaced</u>, so you can <u>use them</u> to work out where the <u>other corners</u> go.

Square
....

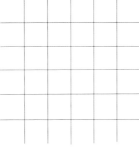

Octagon
....

Pentagon
....

Triangle
....

M...hapes

Make Skele *photocopy* D Shapes

You can make ske... -D shapes using
straws or pipe cl...

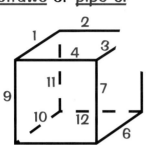

I wish someone would make me a skeleton

We can count <u>12</u> edges on this <u>cube</u> so you'd need 12 straws or pipe cleaners to make a <u>skeleton</u> of it.

How many straws would you need to make skeletons of these shapes?

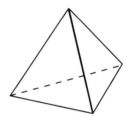

.... straws

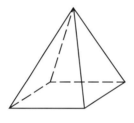

.... straws

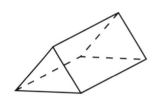

.... straws

Recognise Nets of 3-D Shapes

<u>Unfold</u> these 3-D shapes and you get things called <u>shape nets</u>. If you cut some <u>card</u> into the shape of these nets, you can <u>fold</u> along the lines to make the 3-D shapes.

Match the 3-D shapes to their shape nets — I've done one for you.

The trick is to look at the <u>faces</u>.
1) For each solid object, <u>count the faces</u>.
2) Find all the shape nets with the <u>same number of faces</u>.
3) Then look for the one with the <u>right shapes</u>.
4) If you're still not sure, <u>try</u> making one!

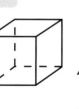

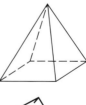

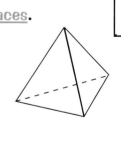

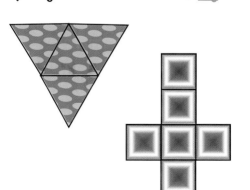

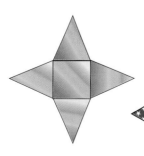

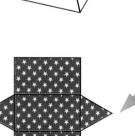

Solving Problems	**Properties of 3-D Solids**

Properties of Prisms and Pyramids

Look at these prisms and fill in the missing numbers.

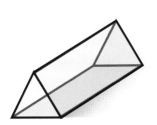 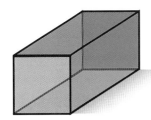 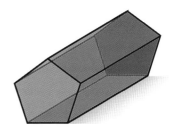 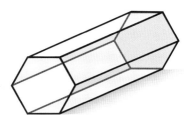

_5_ faces   .... faces   .... faces   _8_ faces

_9_ straight edges   _12_ straight edges   .... straight edges   .... straight edges

_3_ edges on an   .... edges on an   _5_ edges on an   .... edges on an
end face   end face   end face   end face

Look at your answers. The number of straight edges is always a multiple of ....

The number of faces is always .... more than the number of edges on an end face.

Now do the same for these pyramids.

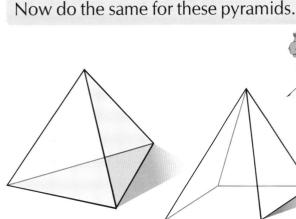 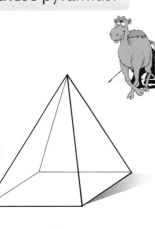 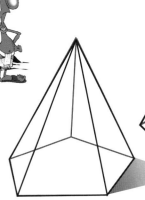 

_4_ faces   .... faces   _6_ faces   .... faces

_6_ edges   _8_ edges   .... edges   .... edges

_3_ edges on base   .... edges on base   .... edges on base   _6_ edges on base

All pyramids have an .... number of edges. (Hint: think odd or even).

The number of faces is always .... more than the number of edges on the base.

Index

Index